Comments

I just wanted to thank you again for your class tonight. You always get me to dance my best. You have built a simple, logical, understandable system, demonstrably superior to anything that this dancing mouse has seen. ~ Erin, social dancer

* * *

I have been a huge fan of your method. Thanks so much for early access several years ago. ~ Paul Hughes, ballroom dance instructor

* * *

I thought your presentation on lead and follow techniques was extremely well thought out and helpful. It would be a wonderful elective activity at workshops like Chagiga and Machol Miami, etc. ~ Rhea, Israeli dance instructor and social dancer

More Comments

For more comments, see the Appendix topic What Others Have to Say at the back of this book.

How This Book Helps You

The Solution to a 1,000-Year-Old Problem

This book solves the biggest problem in social dancing, a problem that affects millions of people. The problem is how to communicate unambiguously. Dance teachers have an enormous wealth of knowledge. However, when explaining how to communicate, they are surprisingly vague. This vagueness is not the fault of dance teachers. Men and women have been social dancing at least as far back as the eleventh century. Until now, there was no clearly defined method for communicating.

Learn the Language for Partner Dancing

This book explains how to communicate every step in every social dance following the three laws of balance, connection, and direction. The method is so simple that the main rules fit on a single sheet of paper which you can learn in an afternoon. You learn to communicate as effortlessly in dancing as you do in speaking.

For the first time, you have a clearly defined language so you know what to do without confusion. You only need to learn how to communicate once. You apply the same principles with every person in every dance. You understand more. You learn faster. Your dancing is easier.

Learn To Dance Gently

You learn how to dance without force. You learn to dance without pushing and pulling. You learn to dance without tension and pressure. The benefits are transformative. You learn to dance safely. You learn to dance naturally. You learn to dance as one with your partner with more freedom to express yourself. You learn to dance as light as a feather.

How To Dance With a Partner

The Gentle Method of Unambiguously Communicating Every Step in Every Social Dance

Invented by

Andrew Weitzen

Bronze Inc.
Gainesville, FL

First Edition, Version 1.0, March 2024
www.PartnerDancing.com

Library of Congress Control Number: 2023932801
ISBN: 978-1-958601-07-5 paperback
ISBN: 978-1-958601-06-8 hardcover with dust jacket
ISBN: 978-1-958601-04-4 ebook

Also
ISBN: 978-1-958601-11-2 audio
ISBN: 978-1-958601-12-9 hardcover Amazon no dust jacket

Cover design by Andrew Weitzen
Original cover photograph of large dancers by LaQianya Huynh

Published by Bronze Inc., Gainesville, FL
www.Bronz.com

ABCDs[SM], Andrew Weitzen[TM], Bronze[TM], Law of Balance[SM], Law of Connection[SM], Law of Direction[SM], Partner Dance Language[SM], PDL[SM], Three Laws[SM], Three Signals[SM], and Weitzen[TM] are service marks and trademarks of Andrew Weitzen or Bronze, Inc.

First pre-release version 0.10 2007 website

Dedication

The most important things in life are determined by luck, the most important being who your parents are. I got lucky. For my parents

Sheldon and Edith Weitzen

Acknowledgments

Thank you to all the people who make recreational dancing possible, organizers, teachers, dancers, musicians, and other supporters. If you have ever thought you wanted to contribute to the well-being of others, you have succeeded.

Thank you to those willing to explore my unconventional ideas. To honor my dance teachers, partners, friends, and those attending my sessions for contributing to my development, and therefore to this book, I have included quotes from them or shared stories about them to name them in some way.

I must specifically mention two people, Erin King and Jeff Subeck, without whom my method would surely lack in quality. Their acceptance of my method demanded that I meet the standards of their tenacious, logical minds. Thank you to Erin for letting me work out my ideas on her, still the best follower I know; and to Erin for editing my original work. Thank you to Jeff for being the first person to put my method into practice from the written word.

Happy dancing,
Andrew Weitzen

Books by Andrew Weitzen

How To Dance With a Partner: The Gentle Method of Unambiguously Communicating Every Step in Every Social Dance invented by Andrew Weitzen - The solution to a 1,000-year-old problem. The most important advance since men and women began dancing together. www.PartnerDancing.com

My Fight With Hospice: A Family Caring for Mom, Witness to the Misuse of Prescription Drugs by Andrew Weitzen - A cautionary tale for anyone caring for family members. "Unique, touching, reflective, homage," Philip Schwartz. www.MyFightWithHospice.com

The ABCDs of Social Dancing

Attitude
Safety: Safety first, do not hurt yourself or anyone else. No force.
Courtesy: Be respectful, do not tell anyone else what to do.
Comfort: Be comfortable, say what you need.
Teamwork: The man invites and the woman completes.
Natural: How people naturally move and interact.
Freedom: Maximize freedom of movement.
Clearly Defined: Logical, precise, unambiguous communication.
Easy: Simple enough for a normal person to learn.
Fast: Fast enough to communicate in time to music.
Universal: Works the same with everyone for every dance.

Balance: Everyone maintains their own balance. Everyone does their own dancing.. Everyone moves their own body parts. Maintain your posture. No pushing and pulling.

Connection: The woman maintains the connection. The woman maintains her frame when the connection moves sideways. At all other times, the woman lets her frame adjust.

Direction: The woman maintains her direction: straight, turn, circle. Stops when blocked or at the end of the connection. Go straight, turn, finish going straight. Stay on your line.

Man's Responsibilities: Keep time with the music. Position the couple on the dance. Initiate the woman's movement.
Woman's Responsibilities: Keep time with the man. Complete her movement.

First Steps

> I do not care what your friends say. I think you are a good guy. ~ Hal Kanter, a good guy

Congratulations on your willingness to explore your dance experience in this unique way. Reread this book often. As your dancing progresses, you will have new insights.

Visit www.PartnerDancing.com

Go to the website now. On the website you can:

1. Pay for this book.

2. Sign up for the partner dancing newsletter.

3. Print the rules.

4. Get additional instruction.

Contents

Contents

How To Dance With a Partner

* * *

Part Overview

1. What This Book Does for You

> Thank you for so much, Andy. You have opened my eyes
> in ways I never could have imagined. ~ Cheryl, Israeli
> dancer

Anyone can dance enjoyably with a partner once you know how to communicate. This book shows you how to communicate so you can make every dance a pleasure.

No Time to Negotiate

> Everyone is telling me something different. How do I
> know what to do? ~ Malissa, beginning Argentine tango
> dancer

When you go social dancing, you dance with a lot of people. You have no time to negotiate about how you are going to proceed. You need a common language that all dancers speak.

The Language for Dancing With a Partner

The method in this book is a language. We will call this language PDL^{SM} for convenience. PDL stands for Partner Dance Language^{SM}. This language is the only explicit language for communicating with your dance partner. You learn to explicitly communicate what you want your partner to do. The language is so accurate you can communicate better when the follower is blindfolded because she is not tempted to use external clues. You learn to speak this language while you dance.

Unambiguous Communication

This language is the only unambiguous method of communicating in social dancing. You learn how to communicate unambiguously so your partner knows what to do without confusion.

Clear Definition of the Rules for Leading and Following

You learn the only clear definition of the rules for leading and following. These principles will transform your understanding of how to dance with a partner.

The Three Laws and Three Signals

Incredibly, you can communicate every step in every social dance by following three simple laws and using just three signals. You learn the three laws of balance, connection, and direction. You learn the three signals that let you communicate each move. You learn how to give and respond to subtle signals instantly. This should be the first dance class you take so you can communicate clearly.

Have Fun

> Hannah asked me to dance then she corrected me. A little while later she asked me again then corrected me again. The third time she asked me to dance, I made up an excuse. ~ Richard, social dancer

Social dancing is about having fun. You have more fun in a welcoming atmosphere. This book addresses all aspects of the communication that goes on at social dancing. The most important thing you learn is how to get along with others.

Embrace Nonjudgmental Dancing

> For me, stress is both physical and psychological. I worry about not performing well enough to suit my partner. It would be nice if we did not judge other people's dancing. If we did not want to dance with only the best dancers. It is like elementary school where people who are not athletic get picked last. ~ Margaret, social dancer

Everyone who goes social dancing is entitled to have a good time without the fear of being judged. You learn the difference between social dancing and performance dancing. You learn to create a nonjudgmental environment for your group. You learn to create a respectful relationship with your dance partner. No matter what your level, you learn to have a good time dancing with people of every other level.

Dance Safely

> I have a shoulder injury. Even slight stress inflames the joint. With many people, my shoulder starts hurting almost immediately. With the method in this book, I can dance all night without any strain.

You learn how to dance safely. You learn how to dance without pushing and pulling. You learn how to communicate through body language without the use of force.

Gentlest Method

> You have the gentlest lead. ~ Rene, vintage waltz dancer

Since there is no use of force, this is the gentlest possible method of dancing with a partner. You learn to dance softly which is a joy for you and your partner.

Improve Your Balance

> You move like a cat. ~ Andrea, Argentine tango
> instructor

You learn how to move so you stay balanced. When you are balanced, you are in control of your body. This gives you the ability to respond to your partner's movement. Only when you are balanced can you communicate completely.

Feel More Comfortable, Confident, and Popular

When you understand the principles of how to communicate, you dance with confidence. You feel more comfortable. You feel more popular.

Dance Naturally

> I can never tell if I am following you or if I am leading
> myself. ~ Esther, West Coast swing dance teacher

You learn to dance so naturally that the woman does not feel she is being led. You simply follow the natural flow of your bodies.

Greatest Freedom of Expression

> You are so musical. I love dancing with you. ~ Rosanna,
> Argentine tango dancer

Since you dance without force, you have the maximum physical freedom of movement. This, along with clearly defined rules, gives you the greatest freedom of expression. You can improvise as your partner inspires you. You can add meaning as the music moves you.

Universal Method for Communicating

> How do you know so many dances? ~ Dina, social
> dancer

You learn to communicate once. You use the same method in all your dancing. We have tested this method on dozens of social dances and countless pieces of choreography. The method works for every dance that we know. Here are some of the dances we tested: Argentine tango, balboa, bachata, ballroom, blues, Cajun, cha-cha, contra, Country Western, East Coast swing, English country, folk, foxtrot, hustle, international, Israeli, Latin, lindy hop, mambo, nightclub two-step, Nordic, polka, round, rumba, salsa, samba, square, Texas two-step, waltz, West Coast swing, Western-style square, zydeco, and many others.

Learn New Dances Faster

> I went to my first class in nightclub two-step. The instructor told me this was an advanced class. He said I could watch. If I felt I could keep up, I could jump in. I jumped in right away. When I rotated to the instructor's partner, she wanted to know where I had been dancing. I was already better than the other students in the class, not because I knew more moves, but because I knew how to dance with a partner.

You learn the skills that apply to every dance. Once you know how to dance with a partner, you learn new dances more easily.

Empower Your Social Life

> I was in South Florida for a week. Friday, I went to Argentine tango. Saturday, I took my sister to the movies. Sunday, I went to salsa. Monday, I went to lindy swing. Tuesday, I went to hustle. Wednesday, I visited

my cousins. Thursday, I went to Argentine tango. Friday, I went ballroom dancing. Afterward, I stayed for West Coast swing, hustle, and country two-step.

Being able to do many dances empowers your social life. You can go out dancing almost every night, meet people, and have fun.

Works Even If Your Partner Does Not Know

That was the most beautiful waltz I ever danced. I felt like I was dreaming. ~ Evan, social dancer

You learn the fundamental principles for dancing with a partner. Even if your partner does not know these principles, they still work for you. Your partner will appreciate them.

Works for Choreographed Dances Too

The method in this book works for choreographed dances too. You learn how to do every choreographed dance whether you know the steps or not. You learn how to dance together so you are not just doing choreography but are two people dancing as one.

Get Powerful Insights Into Your Dancing

You learn new ways of understanding your dancing that you can put to practical use. As you progress, the principles in this book help you understand your dancing more deeply. They continually reveal powerful insights on your dance teachers' explanations.

Easy To Understand

Some local teachers disagreed with my advertisement that Argentine tango, although among the most sophisticated of dances, was also among the easiest. Yet, my beginners were dancing Argentine tango the first day. One of them, who was taking another class at the same time, said, "That was so much fun. I loved that we got to dance."

The method in this book is so easy to understand that the main rules are summarized on a single page of paper which you can learn in an afternoon.

Accelerate Your Progress With the ABCDs^SM

The principles are organized in a simple structure of ABCD, which helps you learn faster. While others are trying to assimilate hundreds of pointers, you see the whole picture in a way you can easily remember. You understand more of what your dance teachers tell you. You are better able to apply what you learn to take your dancing to a new level.

Be the Smartest Dancer in Your Group

The method in this book is built on a logical foundation. A logical foundation gives you the terminology to discuss what you are doing with others. Understanding basic elements guides you in new situations. A logical foundation lets you subject each element to analysis. This provides an opportunity for finding flaws, making improvements, and uncovering new possibilities.

Get Better Each Time You Go Dancing

> Practice does not make perfect. Practice makes permanence. ~ Swing dance instructor

You have to be careful you are practicing skills that make you better and are not reinforcing bad habits that make you worse. This book guides your progress so you know you are practicing the correct skills in the right way. You invest years into the dancing that you love.

As long as you have made this commitment, give yourself every opportunity to improve. Be sure you are learning the skills that help your dancing flourish. Make sure you get better each time you go dancing.

Helps Dance Teachers

This book helps dance teachers by providing a simple explanation of how to communicate. The ABCDs make teaching easier by providing a consistent set of ideas across all dances. Your students are better able to apply what you teach them.

Points To Remember

1. This book solves the biggest problem people have in social dancing, which is how to communicate.

2. You learn the only unambiguous method of communicating every step in every social dance.

3. You learn the three laws and the three signals that let you communicate every step.

4. You learn to embrace nonjudgmental social dancing.

5. You learn to have fun dancing with people of every level.

6. You learn to dance safely, free from injury and stress.

7. You improve your balance.

8. You feel more comfortable, confident, and popular.

9. You learn to dance naturally.

10. You learn to communicate once. You apply those principles in all your dancing.

1. What This Book Does for You

11. You learn faster, understand more, and accelerate your progress.

12. What you learn works even if your partner does not know the same principles.

13. What you learn works for choreographed dances too.

14. Helps dance teachers by providing a simple explanation of how to communicate.

2. Introduction

First, learn to dance. ~ Sheldon Weitzen, social dancer

Welcome to *How To Dance With a Partner*. You will learn to lead and follow every step in every social dance.

First, Learn To Dance

> When I was young, my dad asked me if I was going to a dance at my high school. I said, "No, I do not like to dance."

> My dad laughed at me. He said, "That is like saying you do not like to play the piano. You have no idea what playing the piano is like. You can say you do not know how to play the piano, but you cannot say you do not like playing the piano. The same with dancing. You have no idea what dancing is like. You can say you do not know how to dance, but you cannot say you do not like to dance." He finished, "First, learn to dance then you can say you do not like to dance."

For the last few decades, I have been learning to dance. After a fling with disco in college, which I have not gotten over, my first organized dancing was Israeli folk dancing. The first thing I learned was to enjoy the company, enjoy the music, get some exercise, and have fun. Was that four things?

Choreography Is Not the Answer

> We went somewhere else first, but they just tried to teach us a routine. We like what you are doing so much better. You are teaching us how to dance. ~ Tabitha and Don, wedding dancers

Next, I tried salsa, during which the antecedents of this book were born. I made an attempt to document the complex choreography, but the book stalled. How we change as we grow. I like to think my intuition rightly understood choreography was not the answer. This book is the antithesis of rote choreography.

Dance Teachers

Along my way, I have found dance teachers to be excellent. Dance teachers are surprisingly consistent, regardless of the dance they are teaching. This consistency reflects universal truths about how two people move together to music. This consistency includes being surprisingly vague about communicating with a partner. Until this book, there was no set of precise rules defining how to unambiguously communicate in social dancing.

Communication Instead of Choreography

> Nancy took me several times to four different dance studios. I learned more in one class with you. ~ Hank, beginning dancer

When I found myself taking on a leadership role in recreational dancing in my community, I focused on communication rather than choreography. In organizing the mass of information I had accumulated, a logical method emerged. I saw that communicating with a dance partner followed a few simple principles, easily learned by anyone, even novice dancers. I have codified these principles into the method in this book.

Print and Memorize the Rules

If you have not done so already, go to the website, print, and then memorize the rules now. Take them with you when you go dancing.

Refer to them often. Apply them however they make sense to you. This is the quickest way for you to get started. As you progress, you will understand them better. They will guide you.

Complete Method for Communicating With a Dance Partner

This book provides the complete method for communicating in social dancing. Included in this book are all the rules you need. There are no superfluous rules. You do not need to make up additional rules.

Subconscious Communication

> Sometimes you come across an extraordinary follower who can follow nearly everything you throw at her. Whether she knows or not, subconsciously she is using a simple set of rules that allow her to follow so well. Similarly, the best leaders are using those same subconscious rules.

Dancing happens too fast for conscious thought. People communicate using subconscious cues. This book elucidates these subconscious cues into an easy-to-understand language. The extraordinary effectiveness is a testament to the accuracy of the language. Once you understand the language, you can train yourself to communicate as effortlessly in dancing as you speak in everyday life.

Important Insights Explained

This book provides an original, comprehensive explanation of how to dance socially with a partner. Some of the insights you learn include:

1. Definition of social dancing

2. Definition of social dance choreography

2. Introduction

3. Definition of the ten foundational values so you have a clear understanding of what is important for social dancing

4. Definition of the three laws that let you communicate every step unambiguously

5. Definition of the three signals that let you communicate every figure

6. Definition of the man's responsibilities

7. Definition of the woman's responsibilities

8. Definition of signals relative to horizontal and vertical movement so you know when and where to move

9. Definition of woman's line of dance so the woman can dance with precision

10. Definition of the three positions

11. Examination of balance so you understand why balance is the most important skill in dancing

12. Examination of pressure and tension so you understand why you should not push and pull

13. Examination of the two types of horizontal movement so you understand why every step can be communicated unambiguously

14. Explanation of the four basic patterns that make up every figure in the woman's choreography

15. Explanation of why the man can communicate the woman's choreography

16. Explanation of why the woman cannot communicate the man's choreography

17. Guidelines for navigating the dance floor to improve safety

18. Guidelines for etiquette in the social dance setting to make your group more respectful

19. How to communicate unambiguously without using visual clues

20. How to communicate unambiguously visually when not physically connected

21. How to communicate unambiguously in choreographed dances

22. How to communicate rhythm changes

23. How to step for effective communication

24. Rules for connecting and breaking the connection

25. Rules for the woman's choreography

26. Rules for when the woman follows the man

27. Rules for when the woman maintains and adjusts her frame

28. Rules for when the woman stops her motion

29. Rules for when the man waits for the woman

30. Rules for not getting your foot stepped on

How to Use This Book

This is the rule book for how to dance with a partner following Andrew Weitzen's ABCDs method for social dancing. Refer to this book to clarify issues. If you find that needed rules are missing, unnecessary rules are included, or there are logical inconsistencies, the author welcomes your feedback on these, as well as other concerns.

An overview of the method of communicating every step is presented in the chapter Language of Partner Dancing. This prepares you for the details in the ABCD sections. Although each principle you learn is helpful, to understand the method in full, you have to make your way through all the ABCDs. Only then will you know how to communicate every step unambiguously.

This book presents the ideas in the order in which they logically build on one another. Read the chapters in order so you understand why the method works. Any information that is not essential is in the Appendix. This book is divided into these parts.

Part Overview - covers in brief the ABCDs that follow. You learn the objective of social dancing, the main problem people have in social dancing, and the solution to that problem.

Part A for Attitude - establishes the ten foundational values for social dancing. You learn to use these principles to help you apply what you learn in your dance classes.

Part B for Balance - helps you to understand your balance, the most important skill in dancing. You learn the law of balance with the profound implications for how you dance.

Part C for Connection - examines how you connect both physically and emotionally with your partner, the music, and your community. You learn the law of connection. You learn how to use the connection to communicate. You learn how to initiate the woman's movement. You learn the three positions, when to connect, and when to break the connection.

Part D for Direction - covers how to communicate what the woman is to do. You learn the law of direction, the deep revelation that allows you to communicate every step in every dance. You learn the three direction signals. You learn where the woman is to go. You learn how the woman knows to stop. You learn the reasons why you can communicate unambiguously.

Part Skill - continues the subject of balance. You learn the physical skills you need. You learn how to move your body to communicate effectively. You learn how to transfer your weight to control your step.

Part Summary - you have a short review of the essential elements you learned throughout this book.

Appendix - contains the author's bio, the rules list, terminology, and testimonials. There are discussions on a dozen different topics including Choreographed Dances, the Circle signal, Counterbalance, Musicality, Pressure and Tension, and more.

Basic Principles

This book makes extensive use of basic principles to help you understand the reasons behind what you are doing. Pay attention to the principles. They guide you when you have questions. An example of a basic principle is safety first, do not hurt yourself or anyone else.

Key Ideas

Key ideas help you apply basic principles. Understand the key ideas to put the basic principles into practice. An example of a key idea is do not apply force to another person.

Catchphrases

This book makes extensive use of catchphrases to help you remember useful information. This book frequently expresses basic principles and key ideas as catchphrases. The catchphrases help you to focus on what you need to do. Repeat the catchphrases like a mantra. An example of a catchphrase is everyone does their own dancing.

Anecdotes

This book makes extensive use of stories to illustrate the points in the text. Stories bring the key ideas to life reinforcing your memory. The anecdotes when not attributed are the author's.

Quotations

This book makes extensive use of quotations. With the exception of a biblical reference, I have used only those quotes that I have heard. The quotes are from my recollection or possibly my wishful thinking. I may have taken some literary license. In some cases, I have changed the names of those quoted. The use of quotes is not an endorsement by any person of this book. The quotes have not been confirmed by those attributed.

Terminology

Technical terms are defined throughout this book. You can find these definitions in the Appendix under Terminology. These terms are not capitalized within the text because too much capitalization disrupts the English reader.

Points To Remember

At the end of each chapter is a list of the most important Points To Remember. Make sure you understand these before proceeding. Use these to review the material in the book.

Text Formatting

Each chapter starts with a heading for the subject of the chapter. The heading is followed by a quotation in offset text. Throughout the chapter are topic headings. Under the topic headings, in offset text may appear rules, definitions, basic principles, key ideas, catchphrases, anecdotes, and quotations. Lastly, in plain text, the author discusses the topic.

Read This Book More than Once

The topic headings throughout each chapter help you skim through the book. Each time you read the book, as your dancing progresses, you will have new insights. If you do not understand something, wait. When you are ready, what you missed will make sense. Like learning anything new, do not try to get everything. Try to get anything.

Learning to Dance is Only a Matter of Time

Training your body to dance takes time. For new dancers, if you dance once a week, you should expect to feel like a beginner for a couple of years. You only get to be a beginner once. Enjoy the process. Remember, everyone who shows up learns to dance as long as you keep showing up. By following the principles in this book, you can be confident that each time you dance you get better by developing good habits.

Keep Taking Classes

> In the salsa classes I was taking, all the women dropped out after level six. The reason they gave, "I just have to follow. I do not need to know any more moves."

Often there are more women than men in the beginning classes. Many women drop out of the classes when they reach the intermediate level because they feel they are only learning patterns. While technical skills should be learned from day one, often in lower-level classes, many students focus on patterns. You should not think you are at a dance class to memorize patterns. The patterns serve as useful pedagogy tools. Focus on skill, not figures.

In higher level classes, there are often more men than women. As the level moves to intermediate and advanced, the instruction moves from figures to technique. Rather than learning more figures, you learn how to improve the quality of your movement, dance more in sync with your partner, dance with more style, and dance with more musicality. The men that keep going to class move beyond the women that drop out. The women that drop out cannot keep up, though they may not know, because the advanced men lead to the level of their partner. Whether you are a leader or follower, if you want to improve, keep taking classes.

Trust Your Teachers

Do not worry about your progress. That is your teacher's problem. If you want to learn to dance, you have one job. Show up to class. Try to be coachable. Eventually, you will be dancing as well as everyone else.

Seek Enlightenment Everywhere

There are wonderful teachers all over the world with an incredible wealth of knowledge. You can learn from everyone, even if you do not agree with everything they are doing. The burden is on you to seek what is right for you when you learn from others. Different people will speak to you differently at different times in your life. On your dance journey, seek enlightenment everywhere.

Small Groups

If you want to learn faster, seek out small groups where you get personal attention from the instructor. The fastest way to improve is with personal feedback.

Group Leaders Need Feedback Too

Your teachers need feedback too. Let them know what they can do to make the dance sessions better for you.

Do the Simple Things Well

The steadiest way to improve is to build your foundation. Work on your fundamentals. You will be well rewarded.

Find Something That is Hard for You To Do

> When I go to a dance class, I am happy when the teacher shows me something that I cannot do. I just found something I can work on for the next couple of years to help me get better.

The adding up of small advancements is how you improve your skills. At some point, you maximize a skill. After that, there is not much room for improvement. When you go to a dance class, if what you are learning is easy, you are only refining something you already know how to do. To get to a new level, you have to find something that is hard for you to do.

Destroy Your Bad Habits to Reform at a Higher Level

> After dancing for years, I felt like I could do anything on the dance floor until I saw myself on video. To my

embarrassment, I looked like a big block of wood. How did that happen? I felt so fluid.

You may be comfortable in your bad habits but they are holding you back. When the music comes on, you do what you always have done. You have to intentionally seek out change. In a sense, you have to destroy yourself to reform at a higher level.

Think for Yourself

> Andy, I find myself using what I learned from you everywhere I can, in the rest of my life too, not just at dancing. ~ Jim Rust, folk dance instructor

Learn from everyone. Think for yourself. People have a tendency to overestimate what they know, including me. I have not done a scientific research study. I am not a professional in biomechanics. The explanations in this book are from my own experience. They are only my interpretation. Still, the method in this book is astoundingly effective. Take these ideas on their own merit. Understand them. Be critical of them. Put them to work for you as you see fit.

Technicalities

This is a practical rule book for social dancers. The descriptions are technical enough for dancers to perform as needed. We have omitted technicalities that are not necessary for social dance instruction.

Repetition

> Tell them what you are going to tell them. Tell them. Tell them what you told them. ~ IBM training instructor

You learn by repetition. This book puts the method of repetition to use. The same principles come up under a variety of topics.

Points To Remember

1. You will learn how to lead and follow every step in every social dance.

2. Learn to dance before you say you do not like dancing.

3. Communicating with a dance partner follows a few simple principles, easily learned by anyone, even novice dancers.

4. This book provides the complete method for communicating with your partner in social dancing.

5. This book elucidates the subconscious cues dancers use to communicate.

6. This is the rule book for Andrew Weitzen's ABCDs method.

7. Print and memorize the rules.

8. Learning to dance is only a matter of time.

9. Keep taking classes.

10. Trust your teachers.

11. The burden is on you to seek what is right for you when learning from others.

12. Seek out small groups to get personal attention.

13. Support your instructor.

14. Work on your fundamentals. Do the basics well.

15. To get to a new level, find something that is hard for you to do.

16. Intentionally seek out change.

2. Introduction

17. Think for yourself.

3. Social Dancing

> Try to be a little charming. ~ Edith Weitzen, social
> dancer and my mother

This book is only concerned with social partner dancing.

Social Dancing Is Social

> Definition of Social Dancing: dancing that puts the social
> nature of dancing first.

While there are many reasons to dance, such as getting exercise, challenging yourself, and entertaining the crowd, at social dancing, you put the social nature of dancing first. You put the feelings of others, in particular your partner, first.

Magic Moments

> Whether at a dance camp, a lindy exchange, or an
> evening social, when most of the people have gone
> home, and the time is late, when there is nobody left to
> see, that is when the best dancing happens. Everyone
> still dancing is loose. You feel a bit delirious. You are
> wholly in the present. You can do something with
> another person you can do in no other way. For a
> moment you become one with your partner, the music,
> and your community.

Like any undertaking, having realistic expectations leads you to better experiences. While magic moments happen in social dancing, if you are depending on the quality of the dancing alone, most of your dances are going to be more sociable than magical. Even if a dance is magical for you that does not mean the dance was magical for your partner. If you are disappointed because the dancing does not meet your standards, you are going to find yourself too frequently an unhappy dancer. Try to have fun with every partner. You can create magic moments with any person if you turn on your charm. While the quality of your dancing may not be any better, the quality of your experience can be magical.

Two People Dancing as One

> Why are you dancing with a partner? What are you getting that is unique to partner dancing? In a word, connection.

The point of dancing with a partner is to dance as one with your partner. You sacrifice everything else for the sake of your partner: how you look, doing the dance properly, and dancing on the beat. None of that matters if you are not dancing as one with your partner.

Dance to the Music

> The violins are on the move. ~ Ney Milo, Argentine tango performer and instructor

What is dancing? Dancing is your expression of the music. If you are just doing steps, and the music is no more than a metronome, then you are marching, not dancing. The artistry is your interpretation of the music through your movement. You must listen to the music, not only the beat, all the music. You connect what you hear to what you do.

The Objective

> Objective of Partner Dancing: two people dancing as one to the music.

While most of your dancing, perhaps thankfully, is not a mystical experience, the objective in all partner dancing, whether performing or dancing socially, is for two people to dance as one to the music. You add meaning to your dancing by responding to your partner. You make your dancing feel authentic by improvising to the music.

A Dance Performance Is for Entertaining Your Audience

> Beth came to my swing classes for years. She followed me to Argentine tango, where our teacher has us work on minutiae that nobody can see, but you can feel. At a ballroom dance, the DJ put on an American tango. Beth ran over to me and said, "Let's put on a show". Performing is not something we normally do, but she was excited, so we danced Argentine tango with a lot of big, dramatic movements.

> At our next tango class, Robert announced to our group that Beth and I got a big ovation for our impromptu tango performance. I said to the group, "It was fun. People like to watch that stuff, but it was about the worst dancing we have ever done."

The purpose of a performance is to entertain your audience. Performance dancing is the opposite of social dancing.

A Social Dance Is for Entertaining You and Your Partner

> Ordinarily, Beth and I never get ovations except from each other.

Social dancing is about having fun with your partner. In social dancing, focus on how you feel. You may be proud when onlookers applaud, but the only people you need to please are you and your partner.

Performance Dancing Is Rehearsed

> I have friends that compete in 10 different ballroom dances. They have been refining the same two-minute routines for a decade.

A dance performance is like a pair's ice-skating competition. The goal in your performance is perfection. You have one partner you know intimately well. Ideally, you get a coach, pick out a piece of music, choreograph a routine, and practice each gesture. You precisely prepare every move ahead of time. You perform a routine that takes only a few minutes. You perform the same routine you practiced. You do not want surprises when you give a performance.

Social Dancing Is Improvised

Social dancing is like playing basketball at the park. You do not know what is going to happen next. You improvise from moment to moment. The goal is for you to have fun. You dance with as many people as you can, some you know well, some you are meeting for the first time. Each dance social lasts up to a few hours. Every dance is unique even when dancing to the same music with the same partner. You respond to your partner and the music. Things go wrong. Social dancing is unpredictable. Surprises are part of the fun.

Learn Communication, Not Chorography

For performances, you need tools that help you perfect your routines. You need tools to keep you on the prepared choreography, preventing deviation. The primary tools are repetition of choreography and familiarity with your partner. This is the opposite need of social dancing. For social dancing, you need tools that allow you to make up the choreography as you go along. You need an explicit language that lets you communicate dynamically with every partner.

Social Dancing Is a Conversation

When you dance socially with another person, you communicate via body language about how the music makes you feel. Like any good conversation, the conversation is unpredictable, ever-changing, challenging, unique, and sometimes messy. That is the fun.

The Challenge in Social Dancing

> I took casino salsa lessons for two years. I got through the highest level, level nine. The problem was, when I went to a salsa club, the only women I could dance with were the ones from my class. I realized I had not learned how to dance with a partner. I had only learned choreography. I was relying on my partners to know the steps.

Your ability to communicate should depend only on your skills. You should not depend on familiarity with your partner nor on knowing the same figures. If you can only do certain moves with your regular partners, you have left social dancing. You have crossed into performance dancing. In social dancing, you need to communicate with people who are not your regular practice partners, some of whom you may be meeting for the first time. The challenge in social dancing is what can you communicate with people you may not know well to express what you hear in the music. To meet this challenge you need a simple, effective language for dancing with a partner.

Social Dance Choreography

> Definition of Social Dance Choreography: any choreography you can unambiguously communicate safely without having practiced with your partner.

All other choreography we call performance choreography. Even with a common language, there is a limit to what choreography you can communicate. A move is leadable in social dancing only if you can theoretically communicate that move unambiguously with someone you have not met before. If your signal is ambiguous, the move is not leadable. If a move is not leadable, you can dance in close proximity but you cannot move as one. You will learn exactly what moves are leadable and what moves are not and why. For those moves that are leadable, of which there are an endless amount, you will learn how to communicate them following the three laws and using the three signals discussed in this book.

Gender Bias in Social Dancing

This book is gender neutral. Anyone can dance any role. Be aware there is a distinct gender bias in today's social dances. Cultural ideals of masculinity and femininity are reflected in the roles of leader and follower as well as in the style of many dances. You can explore ways to express yourself outside traditional gender roles. You may have to pioneer your own style. This book gives you the tools to do so.

Leader and Follower Terminology

The terms Man, One, and the pronoun He are synonymous with Leader. The terms Woman, Two, and the pronoun She are synonymous with Follower.

The terms leader and follower can be problematic for a variety of reasons so we also use the term man for leader and woman for follower even though either role may be danced by any gender. We are introducing the gender neutral terms one and two for the two roles. Since the terms one and two are unfamiliar to today's readers, we primarily use the terms man and woman.

Using man and woman allows for the use of pronouns, making passages more readable. This is one impediment to removing the gender bias in terminology. An example is "The leader must be careful not to pull the follower with the leader's hand as that throws the follower off balance." Egad, trying to get through a book like that would make you nauseous. More readable is "He must be careful not to pull her with his hand as that throws her off balance."

Competitions

> I was at a West Coast swing weekend workshop watching the instructors in a Jack N Jill competition where the teachers get paired randomly. One couple was having a difficult time. I had been in classes with both partners. In the man's class, he encouraged us to use a lot of tension and pressure. In the lady's class, she taught with her husband who had a gentle lead using no tension and pressure. The competitors were good dancers, but she was not used to his use of force.

Even though this book does not address performance dancing, the communication method still works. For competitions like Jack N Jills that test communication skills, the method in this book should give you an advantage.

Performances

> I have a friend who was the prima ballerina for the Florida state ballet. When I told her about my method, she said, "We need that too. I do not need the men muscling me around. I can do my own dancing."

When you watch movies with great dance scenes, you can often see men wrestling their partners around. Seems like the method in this book might help them too.

Points To Remember

1. Definition of Social Dancing: dancing that puts the social nature of dancing first.

3. Social Dancing

2. This book is only concerned with social partner dancing.

3. To create magic moments, try to have fun with every partner.

4. Objective of Partner Dancing: two people dancing as one to the music.

5. Definition of Social Dance Choreography: any choreography you can unambiguously communicate safely without having practiced with your partner. All other choreography we call performance choreography.

6. The terms Man, One, and the pronoun He are synonymous with Leader. The terms Woman, Two, and the pronoun She are synonymous with Follower.

4. The Problem and Solution

> Dancing is a language. Your partner has to know the same language as you if you are going to dance together.
> ~ Billy Fajardo, professional dancer, hustle and salsa instructor, judge, organizer, and world champion

If you go social dancing today, you will find that many people push, pull, and nudge their partner about in the belief that this gets their partner to do what they want. The pushing, pulling, and nudging is an ineffective method of communicating. This is not the only thing their partner is using to understand the communication.

People Do Not Know What They Are Doing

> I was watching a salsa video. I knew right away the instructor could not be leading the move the way he said. I replayed his demonstration in slow motion. Sure enough, he said one thing but did another.

How do thousands of people dance together every day? They use subconscious cues that are ingrained in their muscle memory through years of experience. Since they do not know what these subconscious cues are, there is a lot of miscommunication. This leads to experiences that can be, said nicely, improved upon.

You probably do not have a name for the method you are using to communicate. You probably cannot list the principles, rules, and signals of your communication method in a simple, logical format. In other words, while you may be doing something that seems to work, you do not know exactly what you are doing.

The Problem Is Ambiguous Communication

When you lead a move, the question you need to ask is, is my lead unambiguous? How does your partner know what you want her to do? If your communication could mean more than one thing, you are going to have a problem.

When you teach others to lead a move, not only must your lead be unambiguous, but your explanation must also be unambiguous so your students know how to execute what you are teaching. If you use a vague term like energy, without defining exactly what energy means, your students have to work out for themselves what works. This is not necessarily bad if that is what you intend, but not good if you lack the ideas to explain what you are doing.

Ambiguous communication leads to many issues, the least of which is being out of sync with your partner. More serious issues include injuries, bad habits, limited freedom of expression, and discouragement from slow progress. These issues create unpleasant experiences.

Without a clearly defined language, you have to guess what to do. You have to be something of a mind reader to understand what your partner wants. The communication is implicit, not explicit. People seek out regular partners to minimize the guesswork. Too much attachment to regular partners tends to form cliques. This makes your group less sociable. People without regular partners are left watching from the sidelines. Your group may diminish as a result. All from a failure to communicate.

Everyone Has Their Own Ideas of What Is Proper

> A new woman came to our social. I asked her if her husband danced. She said, "I tried to teach him, but he will not dance. I am too critical." The man may love his wife, but when he goes dancing, she makes him feel horrible.

Communicating includes the whole range of communication that takes place at social dancing. The biggest problems are not the technical aspects, but rather the emotional aspects of social dancing. The problem is everyone has their own ideas of what is proper. When people's ideas differ, you may have negative consequences like conflicts with other dancers, people feeling judged, loss of confidence, and people giving up.

Solving the Problem With Choreography Limits You to the People in Your Class

> In this class, our language is our syllabus of figures. You need to know these figures to dance with the people in this class. If you go somewhere else and they do not know these figures, you will not be able to dance with them. ~ Billy Fajardo, hustle and salsa instructor, judge, organizer, and world champion

One of the ways people try to solve the communication problem is with choreography. The choreography solution is inadequate for multiple reasons. One is that to dance as one with your partner, you must coordinate the exact timing and placement of each step which you cannot do by rote memorization of patterns. Figures only give external clues to the movement. To coordinate timing and placement requires communicating through body language. The fallback, once again, is to regular partners. You do not want to limit your dancing to your regular partners. If you go social dancing, you want to be able to dance with everyone. If you go to places other than your regular dance studio, you want your skills to be transferable to those other venues.

Rote Choreography Limits Your Improvisation to the Music

> I was dancing swing, improvising to the music, when my partner, in a sweet way, said, "Do you know the basics of swing dancing? I think some beginner lessons would help you."

4. The Problem and Solution

> I was dancing with another woman from the same ballroom studio. Instead of trying to dance to the music, I just gave her patterns she knew. After that dance, she said to me, "That was the best you ever led."

Some people consider deviation from prescribed choreography as wrong. They may only have learned figures without having learned how to dance with a partner to the music. Dancing is so much fun you do what you have to do to get by, but the quality of your experience suffers. There is a better way to communicate that solves these problems.

The Solution Is Explicit Communication

The best way to communicate is by explicitly letting your partner know what you want her to do. You signal your partner. She knows what to do by following a simple set of rules. When you learn the method in this book, you will be able to explicitly communicate with your dance partner. You will be able to list the principles, rules, and signals that you use to communicate every step. While you need to train yourself to develop the physical skills to consistently put your knowledge into practice, you will know what you are doing.

The Power of a Clearly Defined Language

> "You are pushing me," Soojin scolded me.

You should not underestimate the power of having a clearly defined language. Once you learn the rules, you will have a tool that teachers, students, and your community can use to discuss precisely how to communicate. Once students understand the principles, they can figure things out for themselves. They can correct the teacher when the teacher makes mistakes.

Points To Remember

1. The problem is ambiguous communication.

2. If you cannot list the principles, rules, and signals of your communication method, you may be doing something that seems to work, but you do not know exactly what you are doing.

3. Ambiguous communication leads to many issues including being out of sync with your partner, injuries, bad habits, slow progress, and unpleasant experiences.

4. Regular partners and standardized choreography are inadequate solutions for social dancing because you want to dance with everyone while being able to improvise to the music.

5. The solution is the language in this book, the first and only clearly defined language for social dancing.

5. The Language of Partner Dancing

> Be a good sport. Go dance. ~ Sheldon Weitzen, social
> dancer

This chapter is for those eager to get started putting the ABCDs into practice. Every figure in social dancing is made up of four basic patterns. You can unambiguously communicate these four basic patterns with three signals following the three laws in this book. You can apply this method from reading this chapter alone. Everything in this chapter is described in detail in the succeeding parts of this book.

Everyone Communicates the Same

> Everyone has their own way of leading. You have to get
> used to each guy. ~ Mari, social dancer

We are now going to solve Mari's problem. You only have to learn to communicate once. You lead and follow in the same way with every person in every dance.

The ABCDs

The language for partner dancing is divided into the ABCDs to help you remember what is important. For dancing, you learn best by doing. You need the ABCDs Rules you printed in First Steps. You can also find the ABCDs both at the beginning of this book and in the back of this book in the Appendix topic Rules Pocket Cards. Review and preferably memorize the ABCDs now until you thoroughly understand them.

A for Attitude

The most important aspect of social dancing is getting along with others. While people differ on what is important to them, to dance with a variety of people you have to find values that everyone can agree on.

Safety, Courtesy, and Comfort

Safety, courtesy, and comfort are the three most important values you share with others at social dancing.

Safety first. Do not hurt yourself or anyone else. Do not apply force to another person. You do not know what another person can safely do at any given moment. You might hurt them.

Courtesy is the second value. Social dancing should be nonjudgmental. Do not tell anyone else what to do. Leave instruction for the teacher. Do not give people feedback either. Even good feedback is judgmental. Accept people for the way they are.

Comfort is the third value. You dance for hours at a time. You should be physically and emotionally comfortable at social dancing. Tell your partner what you need to feel comfortable. The difference between courtesy and comfort? If the issue is about them, do not tell them. If the issue is about you, say what you need.

The Three Laws

The language you use to communicate unambiguously with your partner is based on three laws. The first law is balance, the second connection, and the third direction. With these three laws, you can define the movement for the woman for every step in every social dance.

1. The Law of Balance: everyone maintains their own balance.

2. The Law of Connection: the woman maintains the connection.

3. The Law of Direction: the woman maintains her direction.

Violate the Laws and There Are Consequences

> I was dancing in Chicago with a woman who was a champion dancer. She followed everything I did. Her friend, who was just as good, asked me to dance. When I gave her a turn signal, she started to turn, then stopped. She did not know the law of direction. Whoever she regularly danced with expected her to wait for him to stir her through her turns.

These three laws reflect a deep, fundamental truth about how human bodies move together. Even if your partner does not know these laws, the laws still help you. These are laws, not suggestions. If you violate any of these laws, there are consequences. One consequence is you introduce ambiguity into your communication.

B for Balance

Since everyone maintains their own balance, there is no use of force, not even a little, not even a smidgen of tension in the fingertips, none. That means no pushing and pulling in social dancing. Everyone does their own dancing. Everyone moves their own body parts under their own volition.

C for Connection

The connection is the points that are touching your partner. The follower maintains the connection. The leader initiates or breaks the physical connection at his own choosing. There is no pressure or tension in the connection. Any pressure or tension would violate the law of balance.

When you put your hand in your partner's hand, or you put your arm around your partner, there is no pushing or pulling. Your muscles that maintain the connection should be doing the same thing when you step away from your partner as when you connect to your partner. You move freely. You move by your own choice. You move to respond to your partner's movements, not to their use of force.

Frame

How does the follower know when to move her body or just move her arms without moving her body? Your frame is the shape of your arms to your body. Part of the law of connection is the follower maintains her frame when the connection moves horizontally. When the connection has any vertical movement, she allows her frame to adjust without moving her body unless necessary. In simplest terms, when the connection moves sideways, she moves her body. When the connection moves up or down, she moves her arms.

How Do You Get the Woman To Move?

If you are not going to push and pull your partner, how do you get the woman to move? By following the law of connection: the woman maintains the connection. The man moves the points on his body that the woman is touching. The woman must move herself to maintain the connection with the man.

Invitation, Not Coercion

The communication between the man and the woman is one of the man inviting the woman to move. The woman chooses to move if she wants. There is no coercion in social dancing. If the woman does not move in the way the man intends, the man does not try to force her to move. He accepts what she does.

D for Direction

The man moves the connection to invite the woman to move in a particular direction.

Two Movements Are Step and Rotate

When the woman is standing on one leg and her other leg is free to move, there are two movements she can make. One is to take a step in some direction. The other is to rotate over the foot she is standing on. Since these are the only two things she can do, all the woman's choreography must be made up of these two elements. When you learn how to communicate them, you can communicate every step.

Three Signals Are Straight, Turn, and Circle

The man uses the two movements to signal to the woman to move in three directions:

1. Straight

2. Turn

3. Circle

When the woman starts to step, she is starting to go straight in some way, either forward, backward, sideways, or on a diagonal. When the woman starts to rotate, she is turning either to her left or her right. These are the two natural directions that correspond to the two movements of step and rotate.

The method in this book defines a third direction circle. The circle direction is not required but is convenient because the woman circles in many social dances. For ease of reading, throughout this book, we may omit circle at certain points. We may refer only to the two signals straight and turn. Think of circle as a variation of going straight. In most cases, know that you can substitute circle for straight.

How To Communicate Straight, Turn, and Circle

To invite the woman to go straight the man moves the connection in the direction he wants her to go: forward, backward, sideways, or on a diagonal. To invite the woman to turn, the man moves the connection around the woman to her left or right. To invite the woman to circle, the man moves the connection in such a way that the woman starts to walk in a circle either around or away from and back to the man.

The Woman Maintains Her Direction

The woman's rule is to keep going. Once the woman has started to go straight, turn, or walk in a circle, the man no longer signals her. The woman continues on her own going straight, turning, or walking in a circle.

The Woman Stops When She Is Blocked or Reaches the End of Her Connection

The woman stops when she can go no further. She can go no further when the man blocks the woman's direction of movement with any part of his body in front of any part of her body in the direction she is going. Or she stops when she reaches the end of her connection.

The Man Waits for the Woman to Finish

Once the woman is in motion, the man waits for the woman to finish before asking her to do something else.

Woman's Line of Dance

> I went to a ballroom dance. The ladies did not know the most basic things about following. None of the ladies stayed on their line. They all stepped off their line to turn to face me.

When the woman begins to take a step, she is starting to go straight in some direction. She creates an imaginary line on the floor in the direction in which she is going. This line is the woman's line of dance. The woman is to take every step on her line of dance until she is stopped in that direction. When circling, the woman's line of dance is a circle.

Four Basic Patterns Are Go Straight, Turn in Place, Circle, and Turn While Traveling

The law of direction logically implies there are four basic patterns the man asks the woman to do:

1. Go straight

2. Turn in place

3. Walk in a circle

4. Turn while traveling

For the first pattern, go straight, the woman takes every step on her line of dance facing the same way she started. For the second pattern, when the man invites the woman only to turn, she turns in place. The third pattern is the same as the first, except the woman is on a circle. For the fourth pattern, the man first asks the woman to go straight or circle, then adds a turn, to make a traveling turn.

Go Straight, Turn, Finish Going Straight

The fourth pattern, turn while traveling, is made up of a combination of going straight and turning. First, the man invites the woman to go straight or circle. This establishes her line of dance. Then the man invites her to turn. The woman takes each step, including her turning steps, along her line. Her turning steps are half-turns each. Each step is in her original direction. The direction she is facing changes during her turn. At the end of her turn, she may be facing in another direction. Regardless of the direction the woman is facing, after the woman finishes her turn, she finishes going down her line in the original direction. The sequence is go straight, turn, finish going straight.

How To Communicate Every Figure

Essentially, all the man asks the woman to do is to go straight, turn, and go straight and turn. Once the woman starts her movement, she continues moving until she can go no further. While the rest of this book is filled with details, these are the main elements. All the figures in social dances can be done using this simple method.

Transfer Your Weight

To communicate every step, in addition to following the three laws, you also need the technical skill of transferring your weight from one foot to the other. When you walk normally, you fall from one foot to the other. Falling creates a problem in dancing. While falling, you cannot communicate with your partner because you lose control over your step. You cannot alter the position or timing of your step while falling. The way you control your step is by transferring your weight from one foot to the other so you are balanced throughout your step.

For example, when the man steps forward and the woman steps backward, the woman may fall backward, cutting her step short or taking too long a step. She does not know how long a step to take until the man finishes moving the connection. The way for her to see how long a step to take is to stay balanced on her supporting leg until the man finishes moving the connection, then transferring her weight to her other foot.

Points To Remember

1. Use the mnemonic ABCD: A for Attitude, B for Balance, C for Connection, D for Direction

2. Safety first, do not hurt yourself or anyone else.

3. Courtesy, do not tell anyone else what to do.

4. Comfort, tell your partner what you need to feel comfortable.

5. The Law of Balance: everyone maintains their own balance.

6. The Law of Connection: the woman maintains the connection.

7. The Law of Direction: the woman maintains her direction.

8. Everyone maintains their own balance means no pushing and pulling.

9. The man signals the woman to move by moving the connection.

10. The woman maintains her frame when the connection moves horizontally. The woman adjusts her frame when the connection has vertical movement.

11. There are only two things you can do when standing on one leg: step and rotate.

12. There are three direction signals: straight, turn, and circle.

13. Once the follower starts moving, she keeps going until she can go no further.

14. The woman stops when she reaches the end of her connection, or the man blocks her movement.

15. There are four basic patterns: go straight, turn in place, circle, and turn while traveling.

16. When going straight or circling, the woman takes each step on her line of dance.

17. When turning each step is a half turn.

18. Go straight, turn, finish going straight.

19. Transfer your weight from one foot to the other so you control your step.

How To Dance With a Partner

* * *

Part A for Attitude

6. Attitude

> Every person is different. Every dance is different. Sometimes you have an awesome dance with someone. You go back to that person expecting to have another awesome dance and the dance sucks. That is social dancing. Be open to awesome dances. Be open to sucky dances. ~ Christian Campbell, balboa instructor

The purpose of this book is to create enjoyable, social dance experiences. Like so many experiences in life, your attitude plays one of the most important roles.

Why Dance This Way

In this part, you learn the logical foundation for social dancing. You learn why to social dance according to the method in this book. In the succeeding parts, you will learn how.

Let Go of Your Expectations

Social dancing is about having fun with other people. Sometimes the fun is easy. Sometimes the fun is frustrating. You should be able to enjoy social dancing with any respectful person of any skill level. Creating enjoyable experiences takes more than technique. The most important element is attitude. Leave your expectations behind. Try not to be judgmental. Try to enjoy dancing with people who have different ideas from yours about how to dance to the music. Learn to be happy with what your partner is doing. Try to enjoy the opportunity for variety. Accept what life throws your way. Embrace the whole experience.

Change Your Intention To Accelerate Your Progress

When I ran adult volleyball leagues, newcomers tried to hit the ball over the net whenever the ball came to them. I taught them to use three hits, bump, set, and spike. The first to the setter. The second to the side. The third over the net. Without acquiring any new technical skill, simply by changing their intention, they became better volleyball players. They played as a team, had more fun, and could now improve.

Technical improvement takes training, which takes time, often years. Attitude adjustment may take time too, but if you have the desire, much less. You can get immediate results for your dancing by changing your intention even if you have not yet acquired the skills. Whether you are a dancer, teacher, or organizer, by incorporating the ideas here you set yourself and your group on the path to safer, friendlier, and easier social dancing.

Stop Doing the Two Big, Bad Things

In volleyball, there are two big, bad things that ruin the game. The first is carrying the ball. The second is hitting the ball over whenever the ball comes to you. Only when you stop doing those two things can you get better.

In social dancing, there are two big, bad things. The first is pushing and pulling. The second for the man is trying to control your partner. The second for the woman is not following. When you stop doing these two big, bad things, you will force yourself to develop better skills. Make up your mind to quit applying force to your partner. Make up your mind, when dancing the leader's role, to let your follower do what she will. Make up your mind, when you are dancing the follower's role, to follow the leader.

Anyone Can Learn To Dance

> At an Israeli folk dance camp, dancing in front of where Ira and I were sitting, was a woman we knew who had been dancing for years. When she started, if anyone seemed hopeless, that was her. To say she was uncoordinated, was to be generous. Yet here she was doing every step of a complicated dance. We were impressed. Ira said to me, "See, this proves, no matter how awkward a person starts out, anyone can learn to dance."

Social dancing is a wonderful activity you can do for lifelong well-being. You can dance your whole life with benefits for physical, mental, and emotional health. If you are a dancer, you need no convincing. If you are not a dancer yet, now is the best time to start. What is the trick to learning how to dance? Consistently showing up. Even if you feel you have two left feet, if the woman we were watching can learn to dance, you can too.

Points To Remember

1. The purpose of this book is to create enjoyable social dance experiences.

2. Let go of your expectations.

3. Incorporate the ideas here to set yourself and your group on the path to safer, friendlier and easier social dancing.

4. Stop doing the two big bad things. Stop pushing and pulling. For the man, stop controlling your partner. For the woman, stop not following.

5. Anyone can learn to dance by consistently showing up.

7. Ten Values

I do not care how you look. I only care how you feel. ~
Andrea Pham, Argentine tango instructor

Come with me for a moment on the journey of inventing a communication system for social dancing. The first thing we need to do is identify what our system is for.

Everyone Is Entitled To a Good Time

People often get upset by their lack of playing time in basketball leagues. So, when I ran basketball leagues, I ran two divisions. One was the competitive division and the other was the recreational division. In the competitive division, winning was the goal. Teams could organize their roster any way they thought gave them the best chance to win. At the end of close games, they could make sure all their best players were on the floor.

The people in the recreational division wanted to win too, but the goal was for everyone to play. In the recreational division, each person rotated through the game in order so that everyone played the same amount. At the end of close games, who was on the floor was random. Most likely this was not a team's five best players. This did not give the team the best chance to win. This did give everyone a fair chance to experience playing at the end of a close game, and to maybe make the winning or losing play.

Social dancing is like the recreational division. The purpose of this communication system is to give everyone a fair opportunity to enjoy themselves.

Shared Values

What makes social dancing enjoyable can vary from person to person. If you are going to create a communication system that everyone can use, you need to find common ground. You need to specify what you are attempting to accomplish that everyone can accept. One way to do that is by listing the values that are important to you. These values provide objective criteria for measuring the effectiveness of the communication system. While your list may differ, these are the ten values this book uses to help people have a good time.

The words for each value reflect a category of related ideas. For example consideration, nonjudgmental, and respect are included in value number two courtesy. Logical, precise, and unambiguous all fall into value number seven clearly defined. In order of importance:

1. Safety - safety first, do not hurt yourself or anyone else.

2. Courtesy - be respectful, do not tell anyone else what to do.

3. Comfort - be physically and emotionally comfortable, tell your partner what you need.

4. Teamwork - the man invites, the woman completes.

5. Natural - how people naturally move and interact.

6. Freedom - maximize freedom of movement.

7. Clearly Defined - logical, precise, unambiguous communication.

8. Easy - simple enough for a normal person to learn.

9. Fast - fast enough to communicate in time to music.

10. Universal - works the same with everyone for every dance.

To Help You Remember

To help you remember the ten values, group them like this:

1. SCC - safety, courtesy, and comfort

2. TNF - teamwork, natural, and freedom

3. CDEF and U - clearly defined, easy, fast, and universal

Logical Foundation

> A friend was showing me the posture for close embrace in Argentine tango. I said to him, "You are like an acrobat. You cannot expect other people to be able to lean that far forward." While I learned other useful things from him, I knew what he was showing me was not the answer because his posture was too hard for a normal person to be able to do. What he was demonstrating violated the principles of being natural and easy. Rather than spending years going in the wrong direction, I kept looking for another solution for my posture.

When you understand these values, you can make consistent decisions about how to handle each situation you come across. Use these values to guide you as you seek to understand your dancing. These values give you the logical foundation to discuss your method of dancing with others in your community. By discussing what is important to you, your dance community can create a more agreeable atmosphere for everyone.

The first three, safety, courtesy, and comfort, are social values. They might apply to any social situation. The second three, teamwork, being natural, and freedom, are dance values specific to social dancing. The last four, clearly defined, easy, fast, and universal, are communication requirements needed for communicating in social dancing.

You will learn about each of these values in some detail in the following sections. While much could be written on each, we will spend more time on the first four, as they are the most pertinent to your relationship with your partner. We will discuss in detail how to apply these first four values in your social dance experience. We will speed through the last six presuming that you agree with the premise without needing much convincing. This way we can get to the laws of balance, connection, and direction without undo distraction.

Points To Remember

1. Everyone is entitled to a good time.

2. Use the ten values to guide you.

3. Social values - SCC - safety, courtesy, and comfort

4. Dance values - TNF - teamwork, natural, and freedom

5. Communication requirements - CDEF and U - clearly defined, easy, fast, and universal

8. Social Values

> There is no wrong in swing if you can lead it and she can follow it. ~ Margot, swing dance teacher

When you go social dancing with the right frame of mind, your experience is better. Following these guidelines will help you, your partner, and your group have many pleasant evenings. Remember, this is social dancing, have fun.

Express Yourself

> David leapt and danced before the Lord. ~ Book of Samuel

> Exuberant Israeli dancing has a long tradition. David danced unashamedly 3,000 years ago. The tradition of disapproval goes back just as far, as David's wife was displeased by what she thought was his undignified display. David answered her, "for the sake of the Lord who blessed me, I will celebrate."

If you and your partner are having a good time and are not hurting anyone else, do not let anyone tell you there is something wrong with what you are doing. Anyone of any level can interpret the music in their own unique way. Express yourself.

Do Not Let a Little Rejection Spoil Your Good Time

> We were at Disney World waiting in line as usual. My dad was trying to find someone to talk with to pass the time. Most people ignored him including our own family. He would not let a little rejection deter his enthusiasm for enjoying himself. He persisted. Eventually, he found

a like-minded person he could joke around with until our ride started.

Social dancing is social. You have to put yourself out there. One year a person rejects you. The next year they want to be your best friend. This is the way of the world. Whatever your experience level, there are a lot of fun people waiting to dance with you. Keep looking. You will find them.

Charm Those That Appreciate Your Charms

This guy Eddie gave my friend Michael and me a ride to a party. On the way to the party, Michael and I were talking up the salsa classes we were taking. Eddie said, "I dance too, but I do not need any classes. When I dance, the women cannot control themselves."

At the party, Eddie found himself a young woman to seduce. He started dancing on the empty floor motioning for the woman to join him. Eddie was so confident about his dancing and his moves were so outlandish, we were hysterical with laughter.

The woman giggled.

I took a lap around the club. When I got back, I had to give the guy credit. The woman was on the floor matching Eddie crazy move for crazy move. That guy knew where to work his charms.

Talk to those that want to talk with you. Dance with those that want to dance with you. Make friends with those that want to be friends with you. Work your charms where they are appreciated.

Dancing with Security

There are three social values of primary importance for social dancing. They are safety, courtesy, and comfort.

1. Safety - do not hurt yourself or anyone else.

2. Courtesy - be respectful, do not tell anyone else what to do.

3. Comfort - be physically and emotionally comfortable.

Avoid the Three NOs

Correspondingly, avoid the three NOs. There is no falling, no arguing, and no wrestling in social dancing.

Make Friends Everywhere

Follow the principles of safety, courtesy, and comfort. You will make friends everywhere.

Points To Remember

1. This is social dancing, have fun.

2. Express yourself.

3. Do not let a little rejection spoil your good time.

4. Work your charms where they are appreciated.

5. The three social values of social dancing are safety, courtesy and comfort.

6. There is no falling, no arguing and no wrestling in social dancing.

9. Safety

> I never adjust anyone. You can hurt someone if you try
> to move them. Everyone moves their own bodies. ~
> David Salcedo, award-winning yoga instructor,
> flamenco dancer, and my former roommate

Safety is the first principle of any social situation because nothing is
more important than your health.

Safety First

> Principle of Safety: safety first, do not hurt yourself or
> anyone else.

Put safety first. Sacrifice all other aspects of the dance for the sake of
safety. Safety is the responsibility of both partners, both for
themselves and others around the room.

Do Not Apply Force to Another Person

For safety's sake, do not apply force to another person. Be careful.
You do not know what other people's physical limitations are. You
can hurt someone by trying to make them do something they are not
able to do on their own. You can cause them to slip, fall, jam a finger,
strain a shoulder, twist an ankle, wrench a knee, tear a ligament, or
explode.

Everyone Does Their Own Dancing

> I teach a lot of beginner classes. I always start by telling
> them, for safety's sake, there is no pushing and pulling
> in social dancing. Everyone does their own dancing. All
> the beginners accept this without question. To them,
> everyone doing their own dancing is obvious.

Everyone does their own dancing means no pushing and pulling. Not even a little. Not even in the tips of your fingers. None. Zilch. Zero.

Everyone Moves Their Own Body Parts

You move only your own body parts. You do not move your partner's body parts. This is one of those things that seems obvious but many people are moving other people's body parts without realizing that is what they are doing. When you lift your hand, do you lift your partner's hand too? When your partner is turning, do you stir the pot? These things are moving your partner's body parts. Do not move your partner's body parts. Be aware of what you are doing to your partner. Let your partner make their own movements.

Hold Yourself Up, Do Not Be Dead Weight

A common problem is when the woman expects the man to hold up her hands and arms for her. Everyone holds up their own limbs themselves. You do not rest your body parts on your partner. Similarly, when you dance in body contact, you hold up your own body. Do not rest your body on your partner. Do not make your partner carry you around the dance floor.

No Thumbs, No Hanging On

No grasping your partner, not with your thumbs, not with your fingertips. If you are not an experienced dancer, keep your thumbs away from your partner. Put your thumbs on the side of your own hands. Once the music starts, inexperienced dancers tend to bear down with their thumbs on their partners. Do not hang onto your partner. You should be able to move freely. If your partner gets too far away from you, let them go. They may be trying to escape.

Only Do Moves You Are in Position To Do Safely

If you or your partner are out of position, do not attempt the move. You will not be able to do the move properly if you are not properly prepared. You risk hurting yourself and your partner. If you cannot keep up, that is alright. Slow down if necessary. Go at the speed you can comfortably go. Your partner will have to slow down to stay with you. Do not worry if you miss moves. Do not rush. Take as much time as you need to do a move safely. Better to do a move properly slowly than to do a move poorly on time.

Do Not Try To Control Others

If your partner is moving too slow, do you try to physically force your partner through movements? If your partner is moving too fast, do you try to weigh your partner down to make them go slower? If you are doing anything like this, you are trying to control your partner. As long as no one is getting hurt, let your partner do what they will. Do not try to control your partner.

Do Not Physically Help Others

If your partner is not doing the right thing, do you try to physically nudge your partner into the correct position? When you try to physically help others, you do something that is unnatural to your dancing. This confuses the person you are trying to help. Do not physically help others to dance. If your partner cannot keep up, be patient.

Everyone Owns the Space They Are In

The couple that is already in a space owns that space. A couple's space includes the area around them, both front and back, and to their sides in their lane. A couple's area should include the space needed for one person to turn around the other person. Others should leave enough room that you should be able to go around your partner.

When traveling around the room, you can stop. You do not need to worry that other dancers will run you over. You do not need to worry that you will make other dancers mad. You can dance right where you are until you figure out what to do. You own the space you are in. Other dancers must wait for you to clear your space. Good dancers are capable of improvising in their own space until you move on.

Practice Defensive Dancing

Stay in control. Look before you travel somewhere. The man is responsible for avoiding crashes. Both people should watch their partner's back.

Floor Management

The man is responsible for floor management. The man positions the couple on the dance floor, keeping a safe, evenly spaced distance from the couple in front.

Be Gracious

Do not barge onto the dance floor. Before entering the dance floor, catch the attention of the people that you are entering in front of. Wait for them to acknowledge you to let you in.

Dance in Formation

In groups where people dance in organized lines, squares, or circles, dance in formation. The men have the responsibility for creating an orderly formation. Everyone should dance in the formation whether they know the dance or not. The people who know the dance well should dance upfront or in the center. This allows people who do not know the dance to follow people who do know the dance. If you do not know the dance, do not worry that you will mess up others. The first skill in learning to dance is proper orientation. You should be able to orient yourself in formation even if you do not know the steps. Everyone can go right, left, forward, and back. Dancing in formation builds community. Dancing in formation helps those who do not know the dance learn the dance. If you cannot orient yourself and are a danger to others, then you need to get more instruction before dancing in the wild.

Line of Dance

The line of dance is the direction around the dance floor in which the couples travel. The line of dance is typically in the counterclockwise direction. Unless there is a lot of empty space on your dance floor, you should always move forward around the room in the line of dance.

Stay in Your Lane, Do Not Pass

If you are in an orderly dance hall, when traveling around the room, think of the floor being divided into lanes. Each lane being the width a couple needs to dance. For the sake of safety, courtesy, and comfort, stay in one lane. Do not pass people in your lane. If your dance hall has only one lane, wait for the people in front of you to move on. If there are multiple lanes, you can change lanes sideways but do not weave in and out of lanes. The outer lane is the faster lane. On the other hand, if your dance hall is a melee, keep your head on a swivel. Try not to get or run anyone over.

Right-Of-Way

When two couples attempt to move into the same space, both should avoid a collision. The couple without the right-of-way should give way early enough so the other couple can use the space.

The couple moving forward has the right-of-way over a couple moving backward. As previously noted, you should always move forward in the line of dance so this should normally not be a problem. Circumstances being what they will, there may be times where you may want to move backward in the line of dance. The couple behind you has the right to the space behind you. Do not move backward into other couples against the line of dance.

The couple in a lane has the right-of-way over a couple moving into the lane. The couple in the lane to your side has the right to the space in that lane. Wait for the lane to free up before moving in. When lanes merge, the couple to the inside has the right-of-way. Those in the outside lane should give way.

Traveling and Spot Dancing

When some couples are traveling around the floor and others are dancing in a spot, the spot dancers dance in the center of the floor. The traveling dancers dance in the lanes on the outside of the center. A traveling couple can move to the center or stop temporarily in a corner, out of the way of traffic, to do moves in a spot. When continuing on, the stopped couple gives the right-of-way to the traveling couples.

Health

Dancing is an activity that you can do your whole life if you take care of yourself. Warm up. Limber up. Stretch. Breath. Hydrate. Smile.

Points To Remember

1. Safety is the first principle of any social situation.

2. Principle of Safety: safety first, do not hurt yourself or anyone else.

3. Do not apply force to another person.

4. Everyone does their own dancing.

5. Everyone moves their own body parts.

6. Hold yourself up. Do not be dead weight.

7. No thumbs, no hanging on.

8. Only do moves you are in a position to do safely.

9. Do not try to control others.

10. Do not physically help others.

11. Everyone owns the space they are in.

12. Practice defensive dancing.

13. The man is responsible for floor management.

14. Be gracious. Wait for the approaching couple to let you in.

15. Dance in formation.

16. Stay in your lane. Do not pass.

10. Courtesy

> There is more than one right way to dance. ~ Jim Rust,
> Israeli folk dance instructor

People who go dancing are naturally sociable and know how to behave. Still, a section on courtesy is appropriate.

Be Respectful

> Principle of Courtesy: be respectful, do not tell anyone else what to do.

The golden rule applies to social dancing as elsewhere. Everyone wants to be treated with respect so courtesy is the second principle. After safety, put courtesy ahead of other considerations.

Be Considerate

> Social dancing is about kindness ~ Richard Powers, dance historian, teacher, recreator of cross-step waltz

People go dancing to have a pleasant experience. Try to contribute to their good feelings.

Dance at the Level of Your Partner

Consideration for your partner comes first. Accommodate your partner by dancing at their level. Your partner takes precedence over dance moves. If your partner wants you to do something, be agreeable. Challenge yourself to see how enjoyable an experience you can create for your partner.

Do Not Tell Anyone Else What To Do

> There is one teacher in the room. ~ Sabrina Paxmann, professional west coast swing dancer and instructor

Let other people work out things for themselves. The best way you can help someone else is to dance well yourself. Take the pledge. Say the words, "I pledge not to tell anyone else what to do." If you accept this pledge, let us move on. If you think that telling other people what to do is alright for you, see the Appendix topic Do Not Tell Others What To Do.

You Owe That Person a Dance

If you cannot control yourself, and you tell someone else what to do, the rule is you owe them a dance, you do the asking. Asking someone to dance mitigates some of your criticism but does not permit you to keep telling them what to do.

Do Not Ask, Do Not Tell

Do not ask your partner about your dancing. Ask the teacher. If someone asks you what to do, refer them to the teacher, or offer to practice with them afterward. Even though you think you can help, you cannot help them in someone else's class or at a dance social.

Be Careful About Complimenting People on Their Dancing

Complimenting someone on their dancing comes with a surprising set of issues. The first problem is that when you praise someone you are judging them. Another problem is that the compliment may be inadvertently backhanded, such as, "Your dancing has gotten so much better." The other person may take that to mean you did not like dancing with them in the past. If you must say something about the dance, say something about yourself, like "That was fun."

No Talking

> Do you want to dance, or do you want to talk?

When the music is on, there is no talking. The no talking policy applies to everyone, including the teacher. When the music is on, everyone just dances. If there are issues that need verbal addressing, let the teacher know. The teacher can go over the questions between songs. Everyone is the enforcer of the no talking policy. If someone tries to talk to you while the music is on, put your finger to your lips to shush them.

Greet People When They Arrive

> After my basketball game was over, I got to Israeli dancing late. I saw a new guy there. I asked my cousin who he was. She said, "I do not know. I was going to talk to him after dancing."
>
> I was surprised because my cousin knew better. I scolded her, "That means the poor guy has to hang out the whole night feeling unwelcome. You should have spoken to him first thing." We went over then to meet him.

When you get to the dance hall, greet people. Help new people find partners by introducing them to others. If someone introduces you to a new person, ask them to dance.

Say Goodbye When You Leave

> My roommate Esther got back from dancing one night after I had snuck out early. "Where did you go?" she

scolded me. "Do not leave without saying goodbye. It is not nice."

Do not sneak out of your dance sessions. Say goodbye when you leave.

Getting Dances

While visiting the Washington, DC area, I went to a swing dance at Glen Echo Park. The woman at the desk introduced herself as Debra and chatted with me. She said, "Save me a dance."

There were at least 100 people at this dance, which started with a lesson. Debra and her partner were the teachers. After the lesson I looked for Debra to fulfill my commitment, but she was dancing every dance. This was unusual. Often, the lady teachers sit out a lot because the men are a little intimidated to ask them to dance.

As I was leaving, Debra ran over to me saying, "Hey Florida guy, how about my dance?"

When you go to a dance social, if you want to dance a lot, you have to make yourself available. Position yourself near the dance floor. Walk around the dance floor. Make eye contact with people. Go sit next to someone near the dance floor. Start talking with them. Ask them to dance.

If you do not want to dance, get far away from the dance floor. If you are in another room, away from the dance floor, do not expect someone to ask you to dance.

Dancing Comes Before Talking

People that go dancing are there to dance. Dancing takes precedence over conversation. If you are engaged in conversation when someone comes over to ask you to dance, or you see someone in need of being asked to dance, excuse yourself from the conversation. Go dance. Do not make the other person wait for you to finish the conversation. You can finish the conversation later.

Do You Want To Dance?

> If she says no without a good excuse, I do not ask her again. ~ David, ballroom dancer

If someone asks you to dance, you have three choices. The first choice is "Yes, I would love to dance."

The second choice is you cannot dance at that moment, but you make plans to dance soon after. "Yes, I would love to dance, but I am leaving now. Let us dance first next time. I will come get you."

Your third choice is to say no without making plans. "Thanks, but I am sitting this one out." What that means to the other person is, "I do not want to dance with you. Do not ask me again." If you ever want to dance with that person in the future, you may have to do the asking. Do not expect that person to ask you again.

Before you turn someone down because of their lack of skill, know that future, advanced dancers, start as beginners. You make a good investment by investing in the future.

Share the Wealth

> My procedure is to try to dance with everyone who will dance with me before repeating. I also try to first ask someone who sat out the last dance.

If you are with your spouse, and you do not want to dance with anyone else, that is sweet. If you do not have patience for people who cannot keep up with you, that is alright too. Otherwise, change partners frequently. Give everyone a fair chance to dance.

Dance From the Beginning to the End of Your Partnership

When you accept an invitation to dance, you form a partnership. Your dancing starts right away. From the moment the man presents his hand to the lady, and the lady puts her hand in his, you are dancing. Walk on the floor at the beginning, and off at the end, following the rules of leading and following in this book. Your dance ends at the point where you separate after the dance is over.

Do Dances You Do Not Know

You should do dances you do not know. You are entitled to dance as much as anybody. Every group needs new people. The organizers want you to dance. They need the money.

Spouses

> Hang in there Honey ~ wife to her husband at a beginning dance class

What could be better than dancing with your spouse, the person you love, and connecting with them on all levels. Many couples do just that. If your spouse is not your favorite dance partner, that is quite common. You will do fine together if you follow these rules under courtesy. Do not tell your spouse what to do. Encourage, not criticize. Try to make your spouse your favorite dance partner by having fun with them the way they are.

Hygiene

When you go out social dancing, you are going to be in people's personal space. There is going to be a mixing of aromas. Try to keep yours to a minimum. Wash before you go out. Put on clean clothes. So many people have told me that they are allergic to cologne and perfume, that you should not wear any at dancing. Bad breath is difficult for a partner to deal with. Watch what you eat beforehand. No peanut butter, onions, or spaghetti sauce before you go out. No garlic the day you go out, or three days before for some. You do well to have a confidant who will tell you when you are ripening or have a big, green chunk of spinach in your teeth. Oh yeah, brush your teeth.

Grooming and Attire

> As we were getting ready to go out folk dancing, my friend lamented, "I cannot get the cute gals to dance with me." He was wearing the same clothes he wears to play basketball. He had on gym shorts, a ratty t-shirt with holes, floppy socks, and dirty sneakers. He had not showered. His hair was greasy and questionably combed.

When you dance with a partner, you are in their face. Try to make yourself somewhat appealing. You do not have to look like a movie star. Do what you can with what you have. The important thing is not how good-looking you are, but that you are respectfully groomed. You are going out for a classy evening. Create a good impression. Try not to be the worst dressed, smelliest person in the room.

Be Present, No Phones

> When I see a lady looking at her phone, I do not bother her. I ask someone else to dance.

You are going out to have fun with other people at dancing. Be present. Do not look at your phone. If you are not dancing, engage with other people that are sitting out, practice on your own, or relax watching others. Be a positive contributor to the present community.

Support Your Organizers

> At social functions, my Dad used to make me participate.
> I would try to hide because I was embarrassed. I would
> want to wait until I saw a lot of other people doing the
> thing, but my Dad would make me be the first one out
> there. He would say to me, "You have to help out the
> people who are organizing this. You are young, tall, and
> good-looking. When other people see you up there, they
> will join in."

Other people put a lot of their heart into organizing activities for you
to enjoy. Do what you can to help make the programs a success.

Points To Remember

1. Principle of Courtesy: be respectful, do not tell anyone else
   what to do.

2. People go dancing to have a pleasant experience. Be
   considerate. Try to contribute to their good feelings.

3. Dance at the level of your partner. Your partner takes
   precedence over dance moves.

4. If you do tell someone what to do, you owe them a dance, you
   do the asking.

5. Do not ask. Do not tell.

6. No talking when the music is on.

7. Embrace nonjudgmental dancing.

8. Greet people when you arrive. Say goodbye when you leave.

9. Dancing comes before talking.

Part A for Attitude

10. Dance from the beginning to the end of your partnership.

11. If you turn someone down, arrange the next time to dance with them.

12. Give everyone a chance to dance, change partners.

13. Try to make your spouse your favorite dance partner by having fun with them the way they are.

14. Try not to be the worst dressed, smelliest person in the room.

15. Do not look at your phone.

16. Help out the organizers.

11. Comfort

> Tell him what you need. He is not a mind reader. ~ Edith
> Weitzen, social dancer, happily married wife, and my
> mother

You go dancing for two to three hours, often once a week or more. To do anything that much, you have to be comfortable.

Be Comfortable

> Principle of Comfort: be physically and emotionally
> comfortable, say what you need.

After safety and courtesy, comfort is the most important consideration in social dancing.

You Are Responsible for Your Comfort

Tell your partner what you need to feel comfortable. Your partner cannot read your mind. Telling your partner what you need is a courtesy. You are not doing your partner a favor suffering in silence while planning your partner's demise. Your partner wants you to enjoy yourself.

In the prior chapter on courtesy, you took a pledge not to tell your partner what to do. Now you are told you are supposed to tell your partner what you need to feel comfortable. What is the difference? If what you are telling your partner is about you, tell them what you need to feel comfortable. Here are some examples of what you should tell your partner:

1. I get dizzy easily. Try not to give me too many turns.

2. I have a shoulder injury. Can we keep this hand down here?

3. My knees are sore. Can you take small steps?

If what you are telling your partner is about them, leave them alone. Do not tell your partner what they need to do to get better. Here are some examples of what you should not tell your partner:

1. I am confused by your lead.

2. You are off the beat.

3. You are not keeping your frame.

Be aware that your partner may not be able to change. When the music comes on, people do what they do. Change takes time.

Tell Your Organizers What You Need

"That song was terrible. It had no beat," said Richard.

"What are you telling me now for?" I answered. "Tell me at the beginning so I can put on another song,"

Tell your group organizers what you need to feel comfortable. The music may not be loud enough or may be too loud. Sometimes live bands play too fast or too slow if they are not used to playing for dancers. The floor may be too slippery. The room may be too hot or too cold. You might not be getting an opportunity to dance. If you are uncomfortable, do not feel bad because the solution is beyond your control. Tell your group organizers. Do not wait until the end of the evening to complain. Tell them early enough so they can address the issue. They want to know how they can help you. Others may have the same issue.

Physical Comfort

You have to be physically comfortable while you dance. Otherwise, the dancing will not be fun. Eliminate anything that is causing a strain. Take a deep breath. Find a position that works for you.

11. Comfort

Do you find yourself overheating? If so, there is a good chance you are wearing yourself out from the exertion of pushing and pulling on your partner. Remember, do not try to physically control your partner. Dancing is a communication. If your partner does not do the things you want, find a better way to communicate or enjoy what you get.

Emotional Comfort

> I was invited to teach Israeli folk dancing at the University of Florida. In the class were 30 enthusiastic, young women. There was one guy in the class. He was wearing a tight black bodysuit. After the class, the guy said to me, "In another five years I will be ninety." He was eighty-five years old taking a dance performance class with a roomful of college women.
>
> My friend Sheldon Brook said, "It takes that long to wise up."

You need to be emotionally comfortable when you go dancing. Dancing needs to be a place where you relax. Let yourself be in the moment. Enjoy the experience.

Accommodate Your Partner

> In a dance class, I was dancing the follower's role when David said to me, "You are stepping too wide." So, I tried to step smaller.

If your partner asks you to do something, if you can, accommodate them graciously. Your partner is asking you because this is what they feel they need. Do not take offense. Take this opportunity to do something nice for someone else.

Make Mistakes

> Leave your ego at the door. You cannot be perfect and learn at the same time. ~ Nicklaus Hostettler, Argentine tango instructor

Everyone makes mistakes. Mistakes are necessary to improve. If you are not making mistakes, you are not learning something new.

Do Not Dance on Eggshells

> No negative self-talk. ~ Debra, swing dancer

Never apologize for your dancing. No approval-seeking behavior. If someone does not like your dancing, that is their problem.

You Are Where You Are At

> Often I hear people say, "Just do your best."

> My response is, "I am lucky if I can do my average. Half the time I do worse than that."

Remind yourself that whatever you are doing is all anyone at your experience level can do. No one, including yourself, should expect you to do more. If you or someone else expects more, the expectations are wrong not your dancing.

Dance With Confidence

Dance with confidence whether you feel that way or not. If you dance timidly, you will not improve. Be assertive in your movements. Your dancing is clearer for your partner.

Take a Break

> My scuba diving instructor told us, "If you get panicky underwater, stop. Whatever you are doing is causing your anxiousness."

If you get stressed out dancing, stop. If you need to, tell your partner you are overloaded. Take a break. Be aware your partner may also get stressed out. Do not be offended if your partner needs a break.

Points To Remember

1. You go dancing for two to three hours, often once a week or more. To do anything that much, you have to be physically and emotionally comfortable.

2. Principle of Comfort: be physically and emotionally comfortable, tell your partner what you need.

3. You are responsible for your comfort.

4. Tell your organizers what you need.

5. Accommodate your partner.

6. Make mistakes.

7. Dance with confidence.

8. Take a break.

12. Dance Values

> It helps to have an understanding partner. ~ Al Handler, beginning West Coast swing dancer

The three dance values help you dance enjoyably to the music. They are:

1. Teamwork - the man invites and the woman completes.

2. Natural - how people naturally move and interact.

3. Freedom - maximize freedom of movement.

Points To Remember

1. The three dance values are teamwork, being natural, and freedom.

13. Teamwork

> The man invites the woman. ~ Andrea Pham, Argentine
> tango instructor

In this chapter, you learn about the relationship between the partners. To have two happy people dancing with one another, follow these guidelines.

The Man Invites and the Woman Completes

> Principle of Teamwork: the man invites and the woman
> completes.

The goal is to have two people dancing as one. To dance as one is difficult. You need a method that keeps you in agreement. The method is the man initiates what the woman is to do. The woman completes what the man initiated.

Collaborative Relationship

> Partner dancing is a team sport. ~ Bob Rogers, ballroom
> dance instructor

Your relationship is a collaboration. You want your dancing to physically reflect your emotional relationship which is one of equal, mutual respect. Therefore, your physical relationship must not be controlling, but rather invitational. You want each partner to have the option to participate to the extent they each choose. You want the physical relationship to be one of active participation with each person doing their movements on their own. The man invites the woman. The woman chooses to respond.

Force Changes the Relationship From Collaborative To Coercive

Some people take leading and following to mean the man guides the woman. This is one of the reasons the terms leader and follower are problematic. Thousands, maybe millions, of people dance this way. How do they get their partner to do what they want? The man may turn his hand one way and another to nudge his partner where he wants her to go. He may even try to physically put her where he wants her to be. Regardless of how gentle he may do these things, even if he manages to do them without overt pushing and pulling, this is bad for many reasons. The reason we are examining now is that the man is attempting to control his partner.

If you use any amount of force, even only a little tension in the fingers, you create a different relationship. When the man uses force, the man coerces the woman. When the woman uses force, she compels the man to drag or shove her. This is not the type of relationship you want in social dancing. You do not want to control your partner. You want to be equally active participants by moving under your own volition.

The Leader's Responsibilities

> Can you step on the beat please? ~ Veronica Lane, professional musician and one of my dance partners

The person going first, called the one or the leader, is traditionally the man. The man's job is to be responsible for the couple as a whole. The leader has these responsibilities:

1. Keep time with the music.

2. Position the couple on the dance floor.

3. Initiate the woman's movement.

The Follower's Responsibilities

The other person called the two or the follower, is traditionally the woman. The woman goes second. The woman's job is to follow the man. The woman completes the team so you are dancing as one. The follower has these responsibilities.

1. Keep time with the man.

2. Maintain the connection.

3. Complete her movement.

The Man Prioritizes the Timing for the Woman

The man needs to be aware of how his movement affects when the woman steps. The man's priority is for creating proper timing for the woman, not himself.

How the Communication Works

The communication procedure is this:

1. The man invites the woman to move.

2. The woman completes her movement.

3. The man waits for the woman to finish.

4. Repeat

The Man Invites the Woman To Move

Through the connection, the man signals the woman to move. The communication signals are one way, from the man to the woman. The signal is what the man asks the woman to do. As you learned in the overview under language, the man signals the woman to move in three directions:

1. Straight

2. Turn

3. Circle

The Woman Completes Her Movement

Once the woman has started her movement, initiated by the man, she is free to complete her movement however she likes within the rules discussed later. This gives the woman the opportunity to express herself. This gives the man a chance to improvise off of what the woman does.

The Man Waits for the Woman To Finish

Once the man has invited the woman to do something, the man waits for the woman to complete her movement.

Do Your Job

You are a team. Like any team, each person has a job to do. Do your job. Do not try to do your partner's job even if you think that will help them dance better. That is not your job. Your job is to do the responsibilities listed above.

Put Your Partner First

Partner dancing is a three-minute marriage. If you put anything before your partner, your marriage is going to suffer, as is your dance. Specifically, if you put the choreography ahead of your partner, you are not going to be able to dance as one. Put your partner first.

Points To Remember

1. Principle of Teamwork: the man invites and the woman completes.

2. The relationship is invitational, not controlling.

3. Force changes the relationship from collaborative to coercive.

4. The man's responsibilities are to position the couple on the dance floor, keep time with the music, and initiate the movement.

5. The woman's responsibilities are to keep time with the man, maintain the connection, and complete her movement.

6. The man prioritizes the timing for the woman, not himself.

7. The woman is free to complete her movement however she likes.

8. The man waits for the woman to complete her movement.

9. Do your job. Do not try to do your partner's job.

10. Put your partner first.

14. Natural

> Your body will teach you how to dance. ~ Mimi Santapa,
> Argentine tango instructor

As you become more aware of your body's movements, you will have many questions about what to do. Use the principle of naturalness as a guide in understanding your dancing.

Be Natural

> Principle of Naturalness: how people naturally move and interact.

You should dance based on how people naturally move and interact. The more natural you are the easier your dancing will be.

Natural May Not Be Normal

You should move in a way that is natural. Be aware that natural may not be the way you normally move now. The objective is to acquire a habit of movement that is ideally suited to your body for social dancing.

Consult Your Body

> After an evening of dancing, when I went to bed, my feet cramped up. I knew I must be doing something unnatural. I had been dancing with my weight over the front part of my foot. When I danced with my weight over the sturdy part of my foot, the cramping went away.

When you apply the information you are learning, if the result is something unnatural, take another look at what you are doing. You should move naturally. Consult your body for the answers.

Force Is Not How People Naturally Interact With Others

When you need to pass someone in a crowded room, you do not push them out of the way, no matter how slight a push. That would be rude. You lightly place your hand on their shoulder to get their attention. Then you ask to get by.

Natural Interaction With Others

> I was walking with a friend. She was walking alongside of me. Her shoulders were in line with mine. She was just the right distance away from me. I pointed out to her, "You are naturally following perfectly."

People naturally know how to coordinate their movements with other people. When you stop pushing and pulling, you can use the natural movement of your bodies to communicate.

You Know How To Hold Hands

You have been holding hands your whole life. When you walk down the street holding hands with someone, if you are a good hand holder, you do not pull them along. If you did, they might complain, "Quit pulling me." You both walk at the same pace, side by side. They walk alongside you out of their own accord. Your hands lay quietly in one another's without any tension. You hold hands the same way in social dancing.

Signal via Your Natural Movement

You communicate by how you move your body. Your interaction should be so natural that your partner does not notice the interaction as something happening outside the dancing.

Points To Remember

1. Principle of Naturalness: how people naturally move and interact

2. Consult your body for answers.

3. Force is not how people naturally interact with others.

4. You know how to hold hands

5. Signal via your natural movement.

6. Your interaction should be so natural that you do notice the interaction as something happening outside the dancing.

15. Freedom

Shake everything. ~ African dance instructor

The more freedom of movement the better able you are to interpret the music.

Freedom of Movement

Principle of Freedom: maximize freedom of movement.

When dancing alone, you have complete freedom of movement. When dancing with a partner, you have certain constraints. Your freedom of movement is limited. You should seek the maximum freedom of movement while still being able to communicate accurately.

Freedom of Expression

Dancing is a physical expression of the music. You are dancing to express yourselves. Anything that restricts your freedom unnecessarily is not good. Tension and pressure restrict your freedom. Yet another reason not to use force. Try not to restrict your freedom to express yourselves.

The prior subject of naturalness and this one on freedom are worthy of longer discussions. However, we have much else to cover, so presuming you agree that to dance naturally with the maximum freedom of movement is good, we will continue onward.

Points To Remember

1. Principle of Freedom: maximize freedom of movement.

16. Communication Values

We push and pull people to get them to do what we want. We have all these fancy names, leverage, compression, tension, but all of that is just pushing and pulling. ~ Mark Traynor, West Coast swing instructor, founder of Floor Play, awarded River City Swing's first Trailblazer award

When you push and pull, you do not have an explicit communication system. You wrestle with your partner. You guess at what they want you to do. This is not a great way to communicate.

Requirements for Communicating

Ideally, you want to communicate explicitly so your partner knows unambiguously what to do. An explicit, unambiguous communication system needs to meet these four requirements which we call communication values:

1. Clearly Defined - logical, precise, unambiguous communication.

2. Easy - simple enough for a normal person to learn.

3. Fast - fast enough to communicate in time to music.

4. Universal - works the same with everyone for every dance.

While much could be written, for the sake of brevity, following is a short explanation of each.

Clearly Defined

Principle of Clearly Defined: logical, precise, unambiguous communication.

16. Communication Values

For you to dance as one with another person, you need to understand one another. The communication must be clearly defined with no ambiguity. The communication must make logical sense so you can figure out what to do. The communication must be precise so you can match the timing and placement of your partner.

Easy

> Principle of Easy: simple enough for a normal person to learn.

Social dancing is done by all kinds of people with different levels of ability. As you explore how to move, keep in mind that social dancing must be easy enough for a normal person to learn to do in a reasonable amount of time.

Fast

> Principle of Fast: fast enough to communicate in time to music.

Dancing happens fast. The average dance speed is 120 beats per minute which is two steps per second. If you are going to dance as one, you need a communication method for how you can signal and respond this quickly. The faster the communication the more time you have to complete your movements and the easier your dancing.

Universal

> Principle of Universal: you communicate the same with every person in every dance.

With a universal method, you communicate in the same way with every person in every social dance every place you go. You only need to learn to communicate once. You use the same method in all your dancing.

Points To Remember

1. Four requirements for communicating are clearly defined, easy, fast, and universal.

2. Principle of Clearly Defined: logical, precise, unambiguous communication.

3. Principle of Easy: simple enough for a normal person to learn.

4. Principle of Fast: fast enough to communicate in time to music.

5. Principle of Universal: you communicate the same with every person in every dance.

17. Leader Attitude

> Do not lean over the lady. ~ Dr. Caroline Picart, ballroom dance competitor and instructor

Be aware of the parts of your body in relation to your partner.

Let the Follower Do Her Own Dancing

Do not try to control the follower. You are not directing or guiding the follower. You invite her to do something by sending her a signal. She either does what you asked or she does something else. Whatever she does, you figure out what you need to do to keep dancing appropriately.

Do Not Instruct the Follower

You cannot help the follower by instructing her. Dancing is a skill. To acquire a skill takes training. The follower can only do what she can do at that moment. She cannot acquire a skill simply by your telling her to do something. If you want to offer to spend hours training her, that is fine. Otherwise, let her be.

Use Your Dancing To Help Your Follower

If you are tempted to instruct your follower, rather than telling her what to do, figure out how you can dance in a way that helps her acquire the skill in question.

Use Your Follower To Help You Get Better

Instead of trying to help your follower get better, use your follower to help you get better. If you cannot get your follower to do something, and your teacher can, take this opportunity to learn the skills your teacher has. If your teacher cannot get the follower to do something that means your follower is not ready. Try something else with her.

Slow Down

Whether by yourself or with your partner, if you cannot do something, slow down. If you are trying to learn something new, you cannot do that new thing in time to music. You have to train your muscle memory. Forget the music. Perform the action repeatedly until the action becomes automatic.

Consider Your Partner's Emotional State

Before you put challenges to your partner, take into consideration the circumstances. Be aware of her emotional state, your relationship with her, whether you are in a class or at a dance social, and so on. Dance at the level your partner can enjoy.

Minimum Communication Needed

Use the minimum communication needed to signal the woman. The woman can then dance freely without interference. Extra signals are confusing.

Give the Woman Freedom

> I love that you give me the freedom to dance. ~ Gina, West Coast swing dancer

Do not worry that the woman will be bored. You do not have to go from one move to another to keep the woman entertained. The less you ask the woman to do, the more freedom she has to add her own interpretation to the music. Create opportunities for the woman to improvise. When she improvises, let her finish before starting a new movement.

How a Man Can Do No Wrong

> I was in an Argentine tango class. One of the women said
> I should be using pressure for a particular move. I told
> her I had made the philosophical decision to dance
> without the use of force.

Move yourself, not the woman. Invite your follower to move. When your follower does not do what you intended, resist the temptation to make your follower do what you want. As long as you do not apply force to the woman, you have nothing to fear. You may not be doing anything else right, but at least you will not be doing anything bad.

Lead What You Want, Be Happy With What You Get

Your attitude plays the most important role in your enjoyment. Lead what you want. Be happy with what you get. Be grateful that a lady is willing to dance with you. That alone is awesome regardless of how closely the outcome meets your expectations.

Dance to the Music

> When I was a beginner, I wanted to distinguish myself in
> some way. Looking at the more experienced dancers, I
> realized I was never going to have better skills than
> them, at least not for a long time. I thought, even if I
> cannot dance better, I can create a unique experience by
> my interpretation of the music. I made the decision to do
> two things: dance to the music and dance without using
> force. Both have served me well.

Your movement in dancing only makes sense when connected with the music. If you watch a video of people dancing with the sound off, they look silly. If you turn the sound back on, they look fantastic. No one else can interpret the music in your own unique way. You can create unique experiences by expressing what you hear in the music. Do your partner a favor, dance to the music.

Points To Remember

1. Let the follower do her own dancing.

2. Do not try to control the follower.

3. Do not instruct the follower.

4. Consider your partner's emotional state.

5. Use the minimum communication needed.

6. Give the woman freedom.

7. Do no wrong by applying no force.

8. Lead what you want. Be happy with what you get.

9. Dance to the music.

18. Follower Attitude

You are leading. ~ Juliana Azoubel, Ph.D., professional choreographer of Brazilian dance

No Not Following

If you are a follower, your job is to follow. If you follow your leader, all is well. Try not to anticipate steps. Try not to guess what to do. Just follow.

Why Does the Woman Follow the Man?

> Anyone who knows anything about partner dancing knows what makes a woman a good dancer is she follows the man's lead no matter how good or bad he is. ~ Mona, hustle dance instructor

You learned the technical reason of why to follow which is so you can dance as one with your partner. While you may suppose this is the only reason, the more important reason you follow is the emotional reason. Whenever you engage with another person, you are going to have times when you disagree, sometimes over important issues. You have already learned that dancing happens too fast for negotiation. To avoid conflicts on the dance floor, each person has their own responsibilities. As long as you keep to your responsibilities and the leader keeps to his responsibilities, you have no conflict. Otherwise, you are going to have a fight. Remember, there is no fighting in social dancing.

Follow Your Man, Not the Teacher

> I am talking to the men. The women are to follow. ~ Billy Fajardo, head judge of the world salsa championships

You are the ones dancing together, so you have to do your best with one another. The person responsible for the couple is the man, not the teacher. Whatever instructions the teacher might give, follow your man, not the teacher.

Do Not Help the Leader

> The man is the captain of the ship. Your job is not to keep the ship from sinking. Your job is to go down with the ship.

Do not help the man. Do not try to fix the man. Do not try to keep the man from making mistakes. Your job is to stand by your man the way he is.

Do Not Instruct Your Leader

While the man has all the responsibilities he can handle, your only job is to follow. Following is hard enough without you taking on the leader's responsibilities too. You cannot help the leader by instructing him. The leader can only do what he can do at that moment. He may already be at his limit even if he does not seem that way. You do not know which of the many things the leader is focusing on. When you tell him what to do, you force him to pay attention to your agenda, not his natural development. When you try to assist the leader, you overload him, stressing him out. This makes him want to quit. When I dance the follower's role, I do not help the leader, even when I am the teacher.

Dance What Is Led, No More, No Less

> "What am I supposed to do, the correct choreography or follow you?" complained Veronica.

> "Follow me," of course.

114

Do not try to help the leader by dancing what you presume to be the correct choreography. Do not try to help the leader by dancing what you think he wants. You will not be helping him to learn to lead. He will not know if he led you or you did the move on your own. The best way to help the leader is to dance what is led, no more, no less.

Stay Put

When you do not know what to do, stay where you are. Do not try to guess where to go. Wait for your leader to signal you.

Be Careful Not To Lead

> There can be only one CEO. ~ Steven Hymowitz, Israeli dancer

As a follower, when you start to lead, there is nothing the man can do. He has to follow you until you stop leading. Only when you are prepared to follow him can he do anything with you again. Have the intention to follow. Make following your priority.

What Exactly Is Leading for the Woman?

> In traveling dances, like waltz, I square the room. I go straight down the side, then make a 90-degree turn. Nearly all the ladies subconsciously curve the corners. After a few steps, the lady is out of my arms. I look down at my frame and ask, "What happened to my partner?"

What exactly is leading for the woman? If you direct or resist, you are overtly leading. Even if you are not doing those things you may be unintentionally leading. Anything you do that is not signaled by the man that affects the man is leading. If you keep time with the music instead of the man, you are leading. If you initiate a step, you are leading. If you alter the connection on your own, you are leading. If you change your frame on your own, you are leading. If you reach for the man, you are leading. If you push or pull the man, you are leading. If you do not properly orient yourself in position to the man, you are leading. If you curve the corners, you are leading. If you are not following, you are leading.

Your Partner May Be Compensating for You

In swing dancing, closed position is a V-shape. When doing a basic in place, women often lead themselves in front of the man when they should stay back in the V-shape. I was dancing the follower role with Metin to demonstrate this mistake. When I led myself in front, I expected to move out of the connection, but Metin is such an experienced dancer that he followed me so we were still dancing together.

As a follower, often you cannot tell when you are leading. Good dancers may compensate for you. Pay careful attention to avoid leading. Be aware of what you are doing.

No Back Leading

I was in a salsa workshop. The teacher's assistant had rotated to me. She was back leading the step. I asked her, "Should I follow you or should I lead the step?"

Women should not back lead men. Even teachers should not back lead. First, many of the man's steps are not leadable. Back leading all of the man's steps is impossible. If you attempt to back lead, there will only be certain steps for which your back leading will work. The rest of the time will be anarchy for the leader. Second, if you are trying to teach a man what to do, keep in mind that dancing is muscle memory. When you back lead, you are training the man to follow, not to lead. Following a step is different than leading a step. When you back lead, you are training the man to do something that he does not do in a social dance. If you want to teach the man how to lead, switch roles. Let him be the follower. You be the leader. Then he can see what experience he needs to create for the follower.

Do Not Dance Figures

Do not dance choreographed figures. Figures are pedagogy tools. You should learn to execute the basic figures of a dance properly. They serve as the foundation for understanding the various elements of a dance, such as structure, timing, footwork, and style. They help you to practice with your partner on how to communicate the elements of a dance.

Follow Signals

When you dance with a partner, follow what is led. The leader does not lead a choreographed figure you learned in your dance class. The leader invites you to move according to the rules you learn in this book. Follow the signals.

Follow the Man's Timing

The man's job is to keep time with the music. If he is off the beat, or cannot keep a rhythm, you still must follow him. Timing is the man's responsibility. If he does waltz to foxtrot music, you do waltz and be happy.

What Dance Are We Doing?

At dance socials, the women sometimes ask me, "What dance are we doing?"

I like to answer, "They are all the same. I am leading and you are following."

As long as you use the method in this book, you should be able to follow the basic steps of every social dance. You can ask what dance you are doing, but the answer is always the same. He is leading and you are following. If you approach dancing in this manner, you can do every dance.

The Answer to Every Question the Leader Asks You

One day I stopped by a Brazilian dance class to hand out flyers. The class was almost over. They were starting their cool-down exercises. Their teacher Juliana invited me to join in. After some exercises, Juliana told everyone to partner up. I was with Juliana. The music was playing. There she was in my arms. I asked her, "What are we doing?"

Juliana said, "I do not know. You are leading."

When your leader asks you a question, whether the question has to do with what the instructor said, what exercise you are doing, or if you want to go out Saturday night, the answer is always the same, "I do not know. You are leading".

Why Spend So Much Time Telling Followers To Follow?

I helped out in Kay's novice ballroom class at the fitness center. Kay always says the followers must follow, yet two seconds later, half the wives are telling their husbands what to do.

Why did we spend so much time telling followers to follow? Because followers do not follow. If you do not follow, there is no point in moving on to learn how to communicate. Whenever you are not following, you will not be dancing with your partner. Every book on partner dancing and every teacher of partner dancing says followers must follow. Yet they do not and not just novices. What should you do? Follow your leader.

No Showing Off

> In my tango class, the teacher put on a cha-cha. One of our newer dancers was a champion ballroom dancer. She asked me if I knew cha-cha, which I do. We danced. She threw everything she had learned from tango out the window. She was pushing, pulling, and leading herself through figures. She looked fantastic but she was not following.

Not following is common at every level all the way up to the top. If you are an excellent performer and people are watching, you may be tempted to live up to their expectations. This is not possible without your regular partner. Do not try to show off with an unfamiliar partner. Show off by being gracious to your current partner.

Be Aware of the Habits You Acquired From Your Regular Partner

> I was dancing West Coast swing with a professional. I was having a difficult time. She was a gracious, beautiful dancer. The problem was she was so used to dancing with her regular partner that she was unaware she was not following. She was turning her hand over and back like some guys do but not me. She anticipated certain moves even though I led others.

If you have a regular partner, you have acquired a bunch of habits to dance with him. Be aware of what these habits are. When you struggle with another partner, look to your own habits. Do not expect your other partners to dance like your regular partner. They will not. As a follower, you need to develop the skill to follow all your leaders.

If You Follow, Even Beginners Can Dance

> At my first round dance, Doree said to me, "That was amazing. How did you and Soojin pick up the dances so fast?"

> "Lucky for me Soojin does not know how to round dance so she had to follow me. When I made a mistake, she made the same mistake." I replied. "Every time she looked at another couple I said to her, 'Do not look at anyone else, follow me.'."

> "We are supposed to follow too," said Doree. "No one does, but we should."

Even those that do not know how to dance can get decent results if you follow. Regardless of whether the leader, the follower, or both of you do not know the dance, you can still dance together, as long as you follow the leader. You may not be doing the prescribed steps but at least you will be dancing together.

Whose Is the Fault When Followers Do Not Follow?

> When a follower tries to help a leader, even if he asked her, I stop the class. I make an example of them. I tell the men, do not ask the women what to do. I tell the women, your job is to follow, not help the man.

If every teacher says followers are to follow, whose is the fault when followers do not follow? What can we do to fix the problem? The fault lies with the teachers. You cannot say once or twice or ten times that followers must follow. Dancing is done by muscle memory. At any indication of not following, you must stop. You must prioritize following. You must relentlessly train following into followers so that following is automatic.

Points To Remember

1. You must follow the leader.

2. The leader is the captain of the ship. Your job is not to keep the ship from sinking. Your job is to go down with the ship.

3. Follow the leader, not the teacher.

4. Do not help the leader by instructing him.

5. Dance what is led, no more, no less.

6. Be careful not to lead.

7. No back leading.

8. Follow signals. Do not dance figures.

9. Follow the man's timing.

10. If the man asks you a question, the answer is, "I do not know. You are leading".

11. No showing off with unfamiliar partners.

12. Be aware of the habits you acquired from your regular partner.

13. If you follow, even beginners can dance.

14. You must relentlessly train followers to follow.

How To Dance With a Partner

* * *

Part B for Balance

19. Balance

> Balance is the most important skill in dancing. ~ Linda,
> Nordic folk dance instructor

Balance is the most important skill in dancing. Make mastering balance a priority to improve your dancing.

Understand How the Parts of Your Body Move

When you stand on two feet, you have a nice base over which you can easily balance. However, in social dancing, you are standing on one foot much of the time. Balancing on one foot is complex because your body is not naturally aligned over that foot. Your hips are at a right angle to your leg. You are like a two-legged table missing one leg. Explore how the parts of your body affect your balance.

Understand Your Balance Relative to One Another

> At a swing dance, I asked a woman to dance. She told me she had never danced before. I told her that was no problem. I took her out on the dance floor. I let her feel how I moved without doing anything to her. In no time, she was able to follow the simple things I did. When she did not follow me, I followed her. Though we were not dancing swing, we were dancing. She was relaxed. Her hands lay comfortably in mine. We had fun.

Adding to the complexity is the movement of your partner. To understand how your movements affect one another, look to your balance. Allow your partner to respond to your movement on their own.

Do Not Throw Your Partner Off-Balance

> When I got back to her an hour later, after she had been around the room, she was a mess. She was hanging on for dear life. Her fingers were grabbing at my hands. She was pushing and pulling with her arms. She was trying to do the swing basic without paying any attention to what I was doing. This is what the other guys had done to this poor gal.

Do not try to force a result on your partner. Balance is deeply innate to your being. Balance affects your every movement. If you have ever had vertigo, you know balance even affects how you perceive the world. Losing your balance could result in injury. When your partner pushes and pulls you off-balance, you get stressed. Even only a few, stressful moments on the dance floor can create bad habits that are hard to correct.

Points To Remember

1. Balance is the most important skill in dancing.

2. Make mastering balance a priority to improve your dancing.

3. Pay attention to how your movements affect each other.

4. Do not throw your partner off balance.

5. Balance is deeply innate.

20. Law of Balance

> You have to learn to control your body before you can dance well with a partner. ~ Jorge Torres, Argentine tango professional

You should be balanced with proper posture on your own. You must maintain your balance without depending on your partner.

Everyone Maintains Their Own Balance

> The Law of Balance: everyone maintains their own balance.

For safety's sake, everyone maintains their own balance. If you are not maintaining your balance, you could fall and hurt yourself. You must be able to dance with people that are not your regular partners, some of whom you are meeting for the first time. Being off your balance is especially dangerous when you are depending on someone you do not know well to keep you from falling.

Off-Balance

> Definition of Off-Balance: you are unable to maintain your proper position by yourself.

You are balanced when you can maintain your proper position by yourself. You are off-balance when you cannot maintain your proper position by yourself.

Balance Is How We Communicate

The method in this book uses balance to communicate with your partner. When you are off-balance, you garble the communication. You will not be able to dance with precision.

You Move in the Same Way by Yourself as You Do With a Partner

When you maintain your own balance, you dance in the same way by yourself as you do with a partner. Your muscles do the same thing whether you are by yourself or with a partner. When you practice by yourself, you can recreate what you do with a partner. Your individual practice trains your muscle memory for your movements in social dancing.

You Move Under Your Own Power

You must use your own muscles to power yourself. You must learn to move on your own without using your partner to get yourself moving. You must learn to maintain your balance without using your partner to steady yourself.

Move When You Feel Movement

> I was dancing with a woman. I felt like I was pushing around a heavy weight. I told her as soon as she felt any movement she was to move. I was surprised how suddenly she was easy to dance with.

When you feel movement, move. Do not make your partner drag you around. Be easy to dance with.

Dance as Light as a Feather

> When I was young, the best compliment was to say someone danced as light as a feather.

You can sum up these guidelines with these same words: dance as light as a feather. Make this your mantra.

Practice Off-Balance Movements Ahead of Time

Any choreography that intentionally violates the law of balance is not social dance choreography. Off-balance movements can be fun. You can do them, and other non-social dance choreography, during social dances, but you should practice them with your partner ahead of time. Off-balance movements require special techniques not covered in this book. Be sure you can do them together properly. Be careful not to hurt yourselves or others when you do them on a dance floor. For more information about off-balance movements, see the Appendix topic Counterbalancing.

The Law of Balance Is a Law

The law of balance is a law, not a guideline. The law of balance has profound implications for the way you dance. Use the law of balance as a powerful tool for applying what you learn in your dance classes to your skills on the dance floor.

Points To Remember

1. The Law of Balance: everyone maintains their own balance.

2. Definition of Off-Balance: any time you are unable to maintain your proper position by yourself.

3. Balance is how we communicate.

4. You move in the same way by yourself as you do when dancing with a partner.

5. You move under your own power.

6. Move when you feel movement.

7. Dance as light as a feather.

8. Off-balance movements must be practiced with your partner ahead of time.

9. The law of balance is a law, not a guideline.

21. No Force

> Have you heard of tension and pressure? They are
> hooey. You do not need them to dance. ~ Joel Green,
> Swing Dance USA champion

Anytime you apply force to your partner you are not maintaining
your own balance. You are counterbalancing. Even if your body is
over your own feet, you are still off-balance because you are
maintaining your position by the force you apply to your partner.

No Pushing and Pulling

> In some places, suggesting dancing without pressure
> and tension is heresy. I am tempted to ask who in this
> room invented pressure and tension. Experienced
> dancers are passing along bad habits that others taught
> them.

Do not push and pull on your partner. When you push and pull you
are applying force to your partner. Pressure, tension, compression,
leverage, give weight, resistance, and other terminology are
euphemisms for pushing and pulling. No matter how light, if you use
force, you are pushing and pulling. No force means you dance without
pushing and pulling.

Even a Little Force Is Dangerous

> At a swing dance, women were tumbling to the floor all
> night. At one point, two women that had fallen were
> sitting on the floor side by side.

Do not apply force to another person. Even a little force can throw
someone off-balance. Being off-balance is bad for your dancing.
When you are off-balance, you are out of control. You could fall, hurt

yourself, and hurt someone else. Balance is delicate. You must be careful not to directly affect your partner's balance. Be aware of the force you apply to your partner. Stop using force.

Any Amount of Force Changes the Nature of Your Dancing

Any amount of force requires you to counterbalance that force by being off your balance. Even the slightest tension changes the nature of your dancing. Even if only your fingertips are pulling back, your entire body is in opposition to your partner.

Why Do People Push and Pull?

> Push, pull, push, pull ~ Old-time instructor at a Swing Dance USA workshop

People push and pull on their partner because that is what other people taught them. Regardless of how many people have passed along bad instruction, applying force to another person without their permission is not good.

Everything Is Only a Communication

> If the woman was on roller blades, you could use force to sling her around. With normal shoes, even if the woman was made of steel from the waist up and the man was a tank, still no amount of force could make her pick up her feet to take a step. You could knock her over. You could cause her to stumble, but you cannot make her dance. You can only invite her to dance.

You are not physically helping your partner to move. You are only sending a signal to which your partner responds. Pushing and pulling is an inefficient method of sending a signal.

21. No Force

Force Creates Ambiguity

In conversation, many dancers often agree that everyone should maintain their own balance. Many dance teachers say the same thing. Few people follow this to the logical conclusion which is no pushing and pulling, not even a little.

You cannot communicate unambiguously using force. Everyone uses a different amount of force at different times. People interpret that force differently. With the use of force, you can no longer unambiguously define the movement of the woman. You cannot communicate with precision where and when to step. You cannot communicate unambiguously whether to step or to increase the amount of counterbalancing. If your communication is ambiguous, your dancing is not going to be in sync with your partner. If you want to dance as one, you need to maintain your own balance without the use of force.

There Is No Stay Put Signal When You Use Pressure and Tension

Perhaps the worst miscommunication with the use of force is there is no stay put signal. If you use pressure and tension when you are in a stationary position, you have no clear definition for the woman to stay where she is. The problem is you are applying a force to the woman even when you do not want her to move. You cannot communicate unambiguously for the woman to stay where she is. If you dance without force, the woman knows not to move because the connection is still.

Force Is Slow

I was dancing with a guy who was a good dancer and a lot of fun. We were able to do all the figures when the

music was slow. When you put on the fast music, I found
I was behind on all the moves. I thought I had reached
my speed limit. When I got to you, I had no problem. It
was easy for me to finish every figure. I realized that he
was pushing and pulling on me, not a lot, but even that
little bit slowed us down enough that we could not keep
up. ~ Erin, in my hustle dance class

Force slows you down for many reasons. Force affects your balance.
When you use force, you go further than your neutral balance. To
change directions, you have to recover from this extra movement.
Force takes time to build up and counteract. Your partner's natural
tendency is to resist the force, delaying their response. Force is an
intermediary signal. The woman has to translate the force into an
action. When the music gets faster, the slowing effect of force
becomes clearer.

The average dance speed is 120 beats per minute, which is two
steps per second. That means you have half a second, or 5/10 of a
second, for each step. If you lose only 1/10 to 2/10 of a second by the
use of force, you lose 20 to 40 percent of your available time. You will
be 20 to 40 percent slower than someone who dances without
pressure and tension.

When You Use Force You Cannot Train on Your Own

I was dancing with a guy who used a lot of pressure and
tension. I noticed the timing for all our movements was
off. We were still on the music but in a different way than
when I dance without pushing and pulling.

When you use pressure and tension, you cannot practice by yourself
in the same way as you dance with a partner. Your balance, timing,
and positioning are different than when you practice by yourself. You
restrict your ability to get better practicing on your own.

Resist the Temptation To Apply Force To Correct Your Partner

If your partner does not have sufficient skill to perform the movement, your forcing your partner through the movement is not going to improve your partner's skill. When you apply force to get your partner to move, you are training your partner to wait for the force to move. You are training your partner's muscle memory to be off-balance. You are training your partner in a bad habit. You are also training yourself in a bad habit. Be determined to resist pushing and pulling on your partner.

Do Not Use Your Partner To Move Yourself

Are you grasping with the tips of your fingers? If your partner is moving too fast, do you hang on to keep up? When you rock back away from your partner, do you pull on your partner to stop moving backward? When you come forward, do you pull on your partner to start moving? When you walk into your partner, do you push on your partner to stop your forward movement? Do you push on your partner to move away from your partner? If you are doing these things, you are using your partner to help you move.

Do not use your partner to help you move. Move under your own power without the assistance of your partner.

Move Your Feet

Last night I went to a hustle dance class taught by world champions Katie Marlow and Billy Fajardo. This class is mainly young retirees looking for a good time. Billy drills them as if they were aspiring professionals. Every word out of his mouth is a gem. At one point Billy barks at them, "People, there is a name for what you are doing and it is not dancing. It is wrestling. Men, do not help the women turn. The women must learn to get around on their own. At the end of the turn, I can see the men flexing to hold the women up. At the end of their extensions, men are yanking the women back. This puts a strain on everyone. Every person must learn to dance on their own."

The answer to a lot of problems you have on the dance floor is to move your feet. Whenever you feel pushing or pulling, something is wrong. Much of the reason you use force is because you are out of position. To compensate, you pull on your partner to try to catch up, but force makes things worse. When you feel force, take that as a message that you need to move sooner, further, and more accurately. Adjust your position until there is no pulling or pushing.

You May Have To Unlearn Years of Training

If you are an experienced dancer, you may have successfully been dancing by pushing and pulling on your partner. You might enjoy pushing and pulling on your partner. Despite the discussion in this book, you may still have trouble seeing why pressure and tension are so bad. Let the ten principles be your guide. Go through each of the ten principles. List one or more ways how pushing and pulling violate each principle. If you violate the law of balance, the method in this book will not work. If you agree to not push and pull on your partner, we can move on. If you still think pushing and pulling is alright for you to do at times, see the Appendix topic Pressure and Tension.

Points To Remember

1. Pressure and tension are force.

2. Force causes ambiguity.

21. No Force

3. Force is slow.

4. Do not apply force to another person.

5. Resist the temptation to use force to correct your partner.

6. Do not use your partner to move yourself.

7. Move your feet.

8. You may have to unlearn years of training.

22. Posture

> Balance is between the ears. ~ Joan Frosch, University of Florida dance professor

Your posture is essential to your communicating with your partner. Good posture enables you to communicate accurately. You communicate by the way your bodies fit together. You are like two puzzle pieces. As long as both pieces lie flat on a table, they fit together. If either of those pieces is raised at an angle off the table, the pieces no longer fit together. As long as you have the proper posture for the dance you are doing, you fit together. If either of you have poor posture, your ability to fit together suffers.

Posture Is the Foundation of Balance

Pay attention to your posture to help you move effectively. Good posture allows your partner to easily dance with you. Depending on the style of dance, your posture may vary. Whatever the style, maintain good posture within that style.

Body Mechanics Are Complex

Your body is made up of a lot of moving parts. Trying to control these parts individually is a daunting task. Maintaining your posture keeps the parts of your body in alignment. Good posture helps your balance making your movement easier.

Everyone Maintains Proper Posture

While proper posture may vary depending on the dance you are doing, everyone should maintain the appropriate posture. If you are unable to do a particular move with proper posture, you should not do that move. Compromising your posture compromises your balance which is unsafe.

The Woman's Posture Defines Her Position

> To demonstrate to a man how to lead the woman to step back, I had him be the follower. I moved the connection for him to step backward. Instead of stepping backward he leaned back. After I told him no leaning, then he had to step back.

You can only define the position of the woman if the woman maintains her posture. As long as the woman maintains her posture, she can only be in one position while maintaining her connection with the man. If the woman alters her posture, she could be in a number of places while still maintaining the connection. Therefore, the woman must maintain her posture so she knows where to be.

Engage Your Core

Your body has a series of bones stacked one upon one another. You need to engage your core to hold everything together. Avoid being a wobbly pile. Do not let your chest sink down. Hold yourself up. No collapsing. Control the movement of your body from head to toe.

Hips in Neutral

> Because of sitting at a desk most people are so tight in their hips I cannot work with them. Their hips are rotated back. I have to send them to a therapist to loosen up their hips so they can get their hips in a neutral position. ~ Jean, personal trainer

You can think of your hips as having three positions. One rotated back, one neutral, and one rotated forward. There may be times in dancing when any of these positions is useful. However, unless you have a good reason to do otherwise, your hips should be in neutral.

Head Over the Body

> For years I tried to improve my posture. My head was forward. Little by little, my posture got better, but I could not get my head all the way over my body. I was still looking at the floor instead of straight ahead. One day in a gym, I overheard a personal trainer tell her client that her hips needed to be in neutral. I rotated my hip forward into the neutral position. A miracle happened. My head was over my body. I was looking straight ahead at eye level.

Your head should be over your body. Your head is a heavy object. Imagine a bowling ball at the end of a pole. When your head is not over your body, your body compensates. This affects your posture. This affects the way you walk. This affects how you signal your partner through your body.

Eyes at Eye Level

Your eyes should be looking at eye level most of the time. When you look up or down, you tilt your head. Tilting your head affects your posture compromising your balance.

No Leaning

Leaning affects your balance. You lose control over your movement when you lean. Leaning is dangerous. Leaning introduces ambiguity into your communication. If you find yourself leaning, this means you did not bring your feet underneath you while maintaining your posture. You lean because you stepped too far away from your partner. Do not lean to compensate for failing to position yourself properly.

Trust Your Posture

Rather than trying to move to the right spot, focus on your posture. Trust that you will move to the right spot as long as you maintain your posture.

Explore Your Posture To Understand Your Balance

Explore the position of your hips, the position of your head, the distribution of your weight on your foot, and the use of different muscles on how they affect your movement. This is complex. Every body shape is different. Get to know yours.

Points To Remember

1. Your posture is essential to your communicating with your partner.

2. Posture is the foundation of balance.

3. Everyone maintains proper posture.

4. The woman's posture defines her position.

5. Hips in neutral.

6. Engage your core.

7. Head over the body.

8. No leaning.

9. Trust your posture to move to the right spot.

10. Look to your body to understand your balance.

23. Step and Rotate

> Never say oops, bluff your way through. ~ Erin King, Israeli dancer

For safety sake, in keeping with the law of balance, you should always have at least one foot on the floor.

Two Horizontal Movements

> Definition of Horizontal Movements: when keeping one foot on the floor, there are only two horizontal movements you can make: step and rotate.

If you stand with one foot on the floor, there are only two horizontal movements you can make. You can take a step in some direction or you can rotate over your standing leg.

All Choreography Is Step and Rotate

Since the only two horizontal movements you can make are step and rotate, all the choreography can be broken down into these two elements. When you learn to lead and follow these two movements, you can communicate every step in every dance.

Step

> Definition of Step: transfer of weight from one foot to another.

A step is the transfer of weight from one foot to another. When you step, you step in a straight line.

Rotate

> Definition of Rotate: rotating to change facing direction without changing weight.

Rotate is changing your facing direction by rotating over your supporting leg. You do not change weight when your rotate. You stay standing on the same leg. As you rotate, your body faces a new direction.

Do Not Step and Rotate at the Same Time

You should not step and rotate at the same time. While stepping and rotating at the same time is possible, this makes you a wobbly top. Stepping and rotating at the same time is bad for your balance.

Two Types of Steps

You can think of two types of steps, a complete step and an incomplete step. Both types of steps are necessary.

Complete Step

> Definition of Complete Step: you finish your step balanced over your supporting leg.

You take a complete step when you move your body fully over your new supporting leg. When you finish a complete step, you are balanced over one foot so you can stop or take another step in any direction.

Incomplete Step

> Definition of Incomplete Step: you finish your step without being balanced over your supporting leg.

When you shift your weight to your free foot, but only move your body part way to that foot, you are taking an incomplete step. The incomplete step includes over movement when you move your body past your supporting foot. When you take an incomplete step, you are not balanced over your supporting leg. You are somewhere between both feet with one or both feet on the floor.

When you finish an incomplete step, you cannot move in any direction. If you are not balanced over both feet, your weight is favored in one direction. Your next step is already initiated in that direction. You will fall toward that direction. If you are balanced over both feet, you are stuck in place. You must shift your weight to one foot or the other before you can step again.

Attempt To Take a Complete Step

When the woman starts her step, she does not know if the man wants her to take a complete step or an incomplete step. The woman should not try to guess at what type of step to take. The woman should attempt to take a complete step each time she steps. If the man wants the woman to take an incomplete step, the man will cut the woman's step short or lead her to an over movement.

Points To Remember

1. Definition of Horizontal Movements: when keeping one foot on the floor, there are only two horizontal movements you can make: step and rotate.

2. All choreography can be broken down into step and rotate.

3. Definition of Step: transfer of weight from one foot to another in one linear movement.

4. Definition of Rotate: rotating to change facing direction without changing weight.

23. Step and Rotate

5. Do not step and rotate at the same time.

6. Definition of Complete Step: you finish your step balanced over your supporting leg.

7. Definition of Incomplete Step: you finish your step without being balanced over your supporting leg.

8. The woman should attempt to take a complete step.

24. Review Attitude and Balance

> If you cannot do a move by yourself, you will not be able do the move with your partner. ~ Jorge Torres, Argentine tango professional

In the next two sections C for Connection and D for Direction, you learn the rest of the language. Before continuing on with connection and direction, review here the most essential elements you learned in A for Attitude and B for Balance that you need for what you learn next.

Safety, Courtesy, and Comfort

Safety first. Do not hurt yourself or anyone else. Everyone does their own dancing. Everyone moves their own body parts. Courtesy second. Be respectful. Do not tell anyone else what to do. Third comfort, be physically and emotionally comfortable. You are responsible for your comfort. Tell your partner what you need.

No Pushing and Pulling

You are learning how to dance without the use of force. Do not push and pull on your partner. Not even a little. Not even in the tips of your fingers. None. Zero.

Leaders

The man invites the woman. The man has three responsibilities:

1. Keep time with the music.

2. Position the couple on the dance floor.

3. Initiate the woman's movement.

Followers

The woman has one job, follow the man. The woman has three responsibilities:

1. Keep time with the man.

2. Maintain the connection.

3. Complete her movement.

Everyone Maintains Their Own Balance

Maintain your own balance. Do not throw your partner off-balance. Everyone does their own dancing. Everyone moves their own body parts.

The Follower Maintains Her Posture

To define the position of the woman, the woman must maintain her posture. No leaning. Move your feet.

The Two Horizontal Movements Are Step and Rotate

There are only two horizontal movements: step and rotate. All choreography is made up of these two movements.

Points To Remember

1. Safety first. Do not hurt yourself or anyone else.

2. Courtesy, do not tell others what to do.

3. Comfort, tell your partner what you need.

4. No pushing and pulling.

Part B for Balance

5. Leader's responsibilities: (1) keep time with the music, (2) position the couple, and (3) initiate the woman's movement.

6. Follower's responsibilities: (1) keep time with the man, (2) maintain the connection, and (3) complete her movement.

7. Everyone maintains their own balance.

8. The woman maintains her posture.

9. The two horizontal movements are step and rotate.

* * *

Part C for Connection

25. Connection

> To dance well with another person, you have to connect emotionally with that person. ~ Teo Bartek, Argentine tango instructor

In the last part B for Balance, you learned to communicate unambiguously you must dance without the use of force. In this part C for Connection, you learn how to initiate the woman's movement. In the next part D for Direction, you learn how the woman completes her movement. First, under connection, you examine how you connect both physically and emotionally with your partner, the music, and your community.

Connect With Your Group

When you go dancing, you go to make connections. The first people you connect with are those in your local group. The people you dance with regularly are among the people that you see most frequently in your life. Make friends with them.

Connect With Your Local Community

There are other groups in your town doing different kinds of dancing. You share a kindred bond with these other groups. Get to know these other groups in your community. Share your experiences with them. Try to do community-wide programs together.

Connect With the Dance World

There are other dance groups like yours all over the world. Travel to workshops where you can meet other dancers. Bring back these experiences to your group. Invite guest teachers to your location.

Connect With the Culture

Whatever kind of dancing you do, connect to the culture that the dance comes from. Embracing the originating culture adds depth to your dance experience.

Grow Dancing in Your Community

Once you are no longer a beginning dancer, take on the responsibility of growing dancing in your community. People have gone to a lot of trouble to give you an opportunity to dance. Give something back.

Other Dance Groups Are Your Friends

Other dance groups are your partners not your competitors. The more people recruiting new dancers the better for everyone. Support every group. Promote the events of others even when they conflict with yours. In many communities, less than one person in a thousand dances. The problem is not that you are competing with other groups for the few people that dance. The problem is the lack of market penetration. Everybody should be dancing. Improve your market penetration to one in a hundred, then to one in ten, then to one in two. There are enough people to go around for all the groups. You need all your groups to support one another to grow your dance community.

Emotional Connection to the Music

Connecting emotionally to the music puts your soul in your dancing. Interpreting the music together creates an engaging dance experience. Listen to the music. Feel the rhythm. Forget about who is watching. Have fun with your partner. Inspire one another. Express yourselves to the music.

Emotional Connection With Your Partner

> For me, dancing is all about the connection with my partner. ~ Rachil Bracha, Israeli and salsa dancer

To dance well, you need to connect with your partner. A wonderful connection can be transcendent. Achieving a wonderful connection can be difficult. To make a wonderful connection with another person takes more than technique. You have to connect emotionally, as well as physically. The good news is anyone of any dance level can connect emotionally. Do not get hung up on the technical dance experience. Have empathy for your partner. See them as someone who came out to have some fun. Have fun with them.

Leave Out the Romance

> You may be dancing with someone else's girlfriend or wife, or someone else may be dancing with your girlfriend or wife. You may be dancing with someone who does not want the same things you do. Most people are there just to dance. You have to connect with that person respectfully. ~ Teo Bartek, Argentine tango instructor

If you are dancing with your spouse or a willing partner, you have the best of all worlds. You can go right on leaving the romance in your dancing as long as you do not gross out the rest of the room. For everyone else, dance respectfully by leaving out the romance. People that go dancing regularly are there to dance socially. While some styles of dancing are decidedly romantic, the person that agreed to dance with you, agreed to dance socially with you, not romantically with you. Social dancing is about having fun, not romance. You should be able to have fun with everyone. You should not be romancing anyone that has not invited you to do so. When you leave out the romance, you can connect emotionally with anyone.

Points To Remember

1. Connect to others.

2. Support your community.

3. Grow dancing in your community.

4. Make an emotional connection with your partner and the music.

5. Social dancing is about having fun, not romance.

26. Law of Connection

> Do not let anyone tell you, you have too light a lead. You cannot have too light a lead. ~ Joel Green, lindy hop and balboa dance champion and instructor

In the rest of this section C for Connection, you learn how to get the woman to move. In the next section D for Direction, you learn where the woman is to go once she starts moving.

How Do You Get the Woman To Move

> I was dancing West Coast swing with a professional. When she got to the end of a move, she pulled on my hand. Since I do not like people pulling on me, I let go. She drifted back away. Normally when I do that followers adjust, but she scolded me, saying I had to maintain the connection, so I accommodated her. In her set of rules, both partners maintain the connection by hanging onto each other.

If you respect the law of balance, you do not use force. If you are not going to push and pull the woman, how do you get her to move? To get the woman to move, you teach her the law of connection.

The Law of Connection

> The Law of Connection: the woman maintains the connection.

The rule you use for getting the woman to move is the woman maintains the connection. To get the woman to move, the man moves the connection. The woman must move to keep the connection with the man.

Physical Connection

> Definition of the Physical Connection: the physical parts in contact with your partner.

When you are touching, you are physically connected. Your part of the physical connection is the points on your body that are touching your partner.

No Eyes When Physically Connected

When physically connected, the woman only follows the physical connection. The woman does not use her eyes to figure out what to do. The woman should be able to follow the connection as well with her eyes open as with her eyes closed. The movement of the man is irrelevant to the movement of the woman. If she needed to respond to what she sees the man doing, this would limit what the man could do. The one exception to this is the woman uses her eyes to respond to a presentation of connection.

Presentation of Connection

> Rule of Connection Presentation: when the man presents a connection, he invites the woman to connect.

The man may present a connection for the woman to join. He may present his open hand to the woman, or present another connection in some other obvious way. When the man presents a connection, the woman then makes the connection. The woman connects in the way that makes the most logical sense. The man may make the presentation when the couples are not touching or when the couples are already connected in some other way. The presentation of connection may be a visual cue from the man to the woman. The man cannot expect the woman to necessarily see the presentation. When already physically connected, the woman should be aware of the possibility of the man making a presentation of connection.

The Man Chooses When To Make and Break the Connection

> Rule of Connection Making and Breaking: the man chooses when to make and break the connection.

Anytime the woman makes or breaks the connection on her own, she is not following.

Making Connection

The man either makes the connection by connecting with the woman or the man presents a connection for the woman to join.

Keep Your Hands Available

The woman does not initiate the connection. The woman keeps her hands available for the man allowing the man to make the connection.

No Reaching, No Grabbing, No Fiddling

To connect, you come together comfortably. Maintain your posture, your frame, and your timing. Do not reach for your partner. Reaching is confusing. No grabbing. Your partner may want to avoid you. No rushing. You might collide. No fiddling with the fingers.

When the man approaches the woman, the woman does not reach for the man's hands. She leaves her hands where they are. She waits for the man to take them. She may need to make room by moving her arm slightly to allow the man to place his hand around her back.

Similarly, the man does not reach for the woman. If his partner is out of position, or careening wildly out of control, he does not chase frantically after her. Rather, he calmly places himself where he is supposed to be. He presents the connection. He waits for her to join him.

No Pressure or Tension in the Connection

There is no pressure or tension in the physical connection. When you connect physically, your muscles do the same thing as when you are standing by yourself. Your muscles hold up your own body parts without applying force to your partner.

Unambiguous Signal To Stay Still

When you are stationary, you should feel no sensation of movement in the connection. The connection should be still. With the connection being still, this is an unambiguous signal for the woman to stay where she is.

Moving the Connection

You only move your part of the connection. You do not move your partner's part of the connection. The man moves the connection by moving the points on his body that make up the connection. The man does nothing to the woman. He does not move her body parts. He does not apply force to her. If she is in his way, he can move the connection into her in which case she will need to get out of the way, but he does not push her. He just moves his own body.

Maintaining the Connection

> The man is driving the car. The woman stays in the passenger seat.

The woman maintains the physical connection by moving herself. She moves her body. To maintain the physical connection, the woman must move her feet. The woman does not hang onto the man. She does not use tension to maintain the connection. She must move fast enough to keep the tension at zero. By being in equilibrium with the connection, she knows she is moving correctly. The woman maintains the connection while she is able to do so naturally. When the man moves the connection, the woman continues to maintain the connection as long as she is able to do so as part of her natural movement.

Breaking the Connection

The man chooses when to break the connection. The woman does not break the connection on her own. To break the connection, the man disconnects fast enough so that the woman cannot react to properly maintain the connection. The woman allows the man to break the connection. The woman does not try to maintain the connection by reaching with her hand. The woman has to be careful not to hang onto the man by using tension in her handhold. This makes the connection sticky preventing a clean release.

Your Side of the Connection

You own everything on your side of the connection. You have the freedom to do your part however you like as long as you carry out your responsibilities without adversely affecting your partner. Your partner can only feel the connection. You can do anything you want on your side of the connection as long as you dance as if you are doing what you are supposed to be doing. If you choose to deviate from the basic position on your side of the connection, you may feel something different than what you would normally feel. You need to be experienced enough to know what to do in those cases.

Visual Connection

Definition of the Visual Connection: the imaginary physical connection at a distance midway between the dance partners.

When the physical connection is broken, the woman maintains a visual connection. The woman treats the visual connection as if there were an imaginary physical connection midway between the partners. She uses her eyes to follow the man when not physically connected. Details on following visually are discussed later.

Points To Remember

1. You get the woman to move by following the law of connection.

2. The Law of Connection: the woman maintains the connection.

3. Definition of the Physical Connection: the physical parts in contact with your partner.

4. There is no pressure or tension in the connection.

5. When physically connected, the woman follows only the physical connection. She does not use her eyes.

6. Rule of Connection Presentation: when the man presents a connection, the woman connects.

7. No reaching. No grabbing. No fiddling with the fingers.

8. Definition of the Visual Connection: the imaginary physical connection at a distance midway between the dance partners.

9. When not physically connected, the woman maintains a visual connection.

27. Frame

Frame! ~ Richard Nalli, social dance instructor

You use your arms and body as a tool to communicate. This tool is called your frame. The rules for your frame are part of the law of connection.

What Is Your Frame?

Definition of Frame: the shape of your arms to your body.

Your frame is the shape of your arms to your body. Your posture is part of your frame. The man chooses the shape of both his and the woman's frame.

Soft, Relaxed, Flexible

Tone, not tension ~ Marcos Pereira, Argentine tango professional

Your frame should be soft with a little give like Gumby, not rigid like the Tin Man. A soft frame lets you move comfortably without throwing you off-balance. A flexible frame gives you time to respond to your partner. A relaxed frame gives you the freedom to express yourself.

Move Your Frame as a Unit

While you dance, you move your frame as a unit. You do not just move your arms by themselves. To move your arms, you move your body.

Spaghetti Arms

Your frame changes shape while you dance. You either have frame or your frame is adjusting. When your frame is adjusting, some people say you have spaghetti arms. You need both frame and spaghetti arms each at their appropriate moments.

The Man's Frame

The movement of the man's frame is complex. There is no simple set of rules that define the man's movement. At times, the man maintains his frame. At other times, the man breaks his frame.

The Woman's Frame

> Rule of Frame: when the man moves the connection horizontally the woman maintains her frame. Otherwise, the woman allows her frame to adjust.

When the man moves the connection horizontally only, the woman maintains her frame, if possible. To maintain her frame, she must move her body.

Vertical Movement of the Connection

If there is vertical movement to the connection, even if there is some horizontal movement, the woman lets her frame adjust without moving her position, if possible. If not possible, the woman moves as needed to maintain the connection.

Making Connection With Your Frame

You connect through your frame. You form your frame. You link up by moving your entire body to connect your frame with your partner.

Do not break out of your frame to lunge for your partner. Use whatever time you need to connect comfortably.

Do Not Push With Your Hands

> At Chicago Summer Dance in the Park, I was with a new dancer. She was pushing hard on my left hand which was hurting my injured shoulder. I asked her not to push. She said the previous guy told her to push.

Do not push. New dancers do not know to maintain their frame. They let their frame collapse getting out of position with their partner. As you know, being a courteous dancer, you should not tell people what to do. Other dancers who do not know better, in an attempt to prevent their partner from collapsing their frame, may tell beginners to push with their hands. They are teaching the beginner a bad habit that is hard to correct.

The Feet Are for Moving the Body

> The man cannot reach down to move your feet. Your arms are the steering wheel. You have power steering. When your arms move, you move your feet.

If someone told you to push, one reason is you are collapsing your frame. You may be moving your arms without moving your body. You may not be moving far enough fast enough. To correct the problem, you may need to move further, faster to keep the shape of your frame without pushing.

Loose Frames

> A guy complained that my frame was too loose. I told him my teacher said my frame should be soft. He said he was a teacher too. ~ Tanya, social dancer

If you are a leader that thinks your partner needs a rigid frame, the problem is that you are not aware of how your partner is balanced. You do not know how to move your body to signal to your partner to move. You are not timing your movements to your partner's weight changes. This is normal if you are an experienced dancer that is used to tension. You are used to counterbalancing with your partner. To dance without the use of force, you are going to have to retrain your body to listen to your partner's movements.

Frame Adjustment During Movement

Once the woman is moving, she allows her frame to adjust so she can complete the movement. She does not adjust her frame on her own. When she finishes moving, she returns to frame. The woman is constantly going from frame, to spaghetti arms, and back to frame.

Breaking the Connection From Your Frame

To break the connection, the man must move his part of the connection away from the woman fast enough that the woman cannot maintain the connection. This is easy enough for the man to do by simply letting go of the woman's hand. The woman must not hang onto the man. Remember no reaching, no grabbing, no hanging on. The woman must allow an easy release with no stickiness.

Points To Remember

1. Definition of Frame: the shape of your arms to your body.

2. Your frame should be soft with a little give like Gumby not rigid like the Tin Man.

3. Rule of Frame: when the man moves the connection horizontally the woman maintains her frame. Otherwise, the woman allows her frame to adjust.

27. Frame

4. If there is any vertical movement to the connection, even if there is some horizontal movement, the woman lets her frame adjust without moving her position.

5. Once the woman has started to move, the woman allows her frame to adjust so she can complete the movement.

28. Communicating

> You have to find your center. Everything comes from your center. ~ Katie Marlow, professional dancer, hustle and salsa instructor, and world champion

You can unambiguously define both the position and initial movement of the woman via the law of connection.

Defining the Position of the Woman

The woman's frame and the connection unambiguously define the position of the woman. If the woman maintains her balance, her posture, the connection, and her frame, there is only one place she can be. This allows the man to position the woman wherever he wants by positioning the connection and shaping the woman's frame.

Defining the Initial Movement of the Woman

Moving the woman's frame defines the initial movement of the woman to step or rotate in a particular direction. You can unambiguously define the initial movement of the woman by following the law of connection and the rule of frame. When the man moves the connection horizontally, to maintain her frame, the woman must either start to step or start to rotate in a particular direction.

Initiating the Woman's Choreography Unambiguously

Since you can both define the position and initial movement of the woman, you can unambiguously initiate the woman's choreography for all her steps. Under D for Direction you learn how the woman completes her choreography. You also need the physical skills to be able to communicate in time to the music.

You Communicate Through Your Frame

Your frame transmits the movement of your body. You use your frame to position yourself. You use your frame to initiate movement. The man adjusts his frame to communicate what he wants the woman to do. The woman uses her frame to receive the message from the man.

Connected at Multiple Points

When you are connected at two points or more, the man must move all the points of the connection in a way that communicates to the woman what he wants her to do. If the woman cannot maintain her frame, then the woman adjusts her frame without moving her body if possible. Otherwise, she adjusts both her frame and her position.

Prepare the Woman

To signal the woman to move, the man must move slow enough to allow the woman to follow her rule to maintain the connection. You prepare the woman to move by moving the connection early enough that she can adjust her balance to begin to move with you.

Stillness Means Stay Still

When you do not use pressure and tension, you connect in perfect stillness. There should be no sensation of motion. This still connection is an unambiguous indication to the woman to stay where she is.

Motion Means Move

Whenever the woman feels motion, she moves as directed. The sensation of movement is an unambiguous indication to the woman to move.

Two People Moving in Harmony as One

When you connect without tension, there is harmony between your bodies. When you are still, none of your body parts are attempting to move. When you move, there is harmony in your motion with all parts of your bodies moving together. This is a beautiful thing, like you are dancing.

Communications Are in the Plane of Movement

Rule of Plane of Communication: horizontal communication is for horizontal movement. Vertical communication is for vertical movement.

There are two planes in which you move, horizontal and vertical. Horizontal communication is for horizontal movement. Vertical communication is for vertical movement. Horizontal communication tells the woman which direction to step and which way to rotate. Vertical communication adjusts the woman's arms, as well as raising and lowering her body to stay with the man.

Communicating Step

To invite the woman to step, the man moves the connection in a straight line in the direction he wants the woman to step.

Communicating Rotate

To invite the woman to rotate, the man moves the connection around the woman in the direction he wants her to rotate.

The Sensation Is the Communication

At a West Coast swing dance, one of the women said to me, "Sorry, I could not help myself. I just had to turn."

When the woman moves to maintain the connection, she feels herself stepping or she feels herself rotating. These sensations are significantly different. The woman will not confuse the two. The task of the man is to create the appropriate feeling in the woman.

Focus on Connection

Dancing happens too fast for the woman to think about what to do. The woman must train her body to respond appropriately automatically. The woman should not concern herself with steps. The woman should focus on the connection.

The Woman Should Finely Balance

The woman should be finely balanced able to lightly move as needed. If the woman is finely balanced, any movement by the man invites the woman to initiate her movement.

Adjusting the Position

After coming together, the man may want to adjust the woman slightly from where she is. Any movement the man makes with his frame is a signal to the woman to adjust her position in the direction of movement. When she feels no movement, she is in the correct position.

Raising the Hand Does Not Mean Turn

> Do not be a turn hog. Maybe the man wants to turn once in a while too. Maybe the man has something else in mind.

Raising the hand just means raise the hand. Raising the hand is a vertical movement. Turning is a horizontal movement. To signal the woman to turn, the man must move the connection horizontally. He can signal the turn before or after he raises the hand, not while raising the hand.

Communicating Vertical Movement

To signal the woman to move vertically, the man moves the connection vertically. If possible, the woman moves just her hand up or down to maintain the connection. If necessary, the woman moves her body up or down to maintain the connection.

Coordinate Your Movements Naturally

The man must be aware of how his movement creates a response in the woman. Ideally, he signals the woman as a part of their natural movement. You become one by coordinating your movements through the natural flow of your bodies.

Raise and Lower the Connection

To facilitate the transfer of weight for the woman, the man can slightly raise the connection at the beginning of the step, and lower the connection at the end. The reverse also works, lowering the connection at the beginning and raising the connection at the end.

Slow Down, No Rushing, Prepare Yourselves

> Better never than late. ~ Tara Bolker, contra and English country dance instructor

If you do not have sufficient skill to do a particular move in the requisite time, do not rush. If you cannot keep up, let yourselves fall behind. If you are not in a position to do what you want comfortably, skip the move. You must be in the proper position before executing a movement. Slow down. Prepare yourselves. Use extra beats. Take all the time you need to do the movement well. Once you have mastered the movement, you will be able to increase your speed.

Move With Precision

> In salsa rueda class, I was frantically leading the women through the moves one after the other. Then I got to an advanced woman. Dancing with her was like being in the eye of a hurricane. Everything was peaceful. Her movements were contained. We easily got through the moves calmly without rushing.

The reason you have to rush is you are sloppy in your steps. You only have about half of a second to communicate and execute a step. If you waste tenths of a second with your imprecision, you are not going to have time to do what you need to do. Often your teacher can dance fine with both of you, but you and your partner cannot execute the movement together. This is because when you dance with an experienced partner they can compensate for you, correcting for your inaccuracies, keeping you comfortably on time. When you dance with another inexperienced person, you are like the perfect storm with two waves adding to each other compounding your mistakes. Be precise in your movements. Precision improves your balance. Precision lets you dance with less effort. Precision allows you to communicate more effectively.

Points To Remember

1. The woman's frame and the connection define the position of the woman.

2. Moving the woman's frame defines the initial movement of the woman to step or rotate in a particular direction.

3. You can define the initial choreography of the woman by following the law of connection and rule of frame.

Part C for Connection

4. Stillness means stay still.

5. Motion means move.

6. Rule of Plane of Communication: horizontal communication is for horizontal movement. Vertical communication is for vertical movement.

7. To communicate step the man moves the connection in a straight line.

8. To communicate rotate the man moves the connection around the woman.

9. Raising the hand does not mean turn.

10. Move with precision.

29. Free Position

You are not doing anything to the woman. You are manipulating space. ~ Billy Fajardo, professional dancer and instructor

Three Positions

There are many positions you can be in relative to your partner. For communication purposes, all positions fall into one of three categories.

1. Free Position

2. Open Position

3. Closed Position

When you are touching, you are in an open position or a closed position. You learn about these positions in the succeeding chapters.

Free Position

> Definition of Free Position: any position when the man and woman are not touching one another.

The simplest position is the free position so you learn about this first. Any position in which you are not touching is a free position. This is called a free position because you are physically free from your partner.

Making the Visual Connection in a Free Position

Whenever the man breaks the physical connection, you are in a free position. The woman makes a visual connection when she is no longer touching her partner.

Maintaining the Connection in a Free Position

> Rule of Visual Connection: whenever there is no physical connection the woman maintains a visual connection.

When in a free position, the woman still follows her rule to maintain the connection. As long as she is not touching her partner, the woman watches the man. She imagines the connection point as the middle point between the two partners.

Returning to a Physical Connection From a Free Position

To end the visual connection, the man makes a physical connection with the woman. The man either takes hold of the woman or he presents a connection to which the woman joins. Once touching, the woman no longer follows visually.

Leading and Following in a Free Position

For the explanation of how to communicate while you are not physically connected, see the chapter under D for Direction: Following Visually.

Points To Remember

1. There are three positions for communication purposes: free, open, and closed.

2. Open and closed positions are physically connected positions.

3. Definition of Free Position: any position when the man and woman are not touching one another.

4. Rule of Visual Connection: whenever there is no physical connection the woman maintains a visual connection.

29. Free Position

5. The visual connection point is midway between the partners.

30. Open Position

> There are all these little things you need to know that no
> one tells you ~ Steve Littler, Argentine tango dancer

In this chapter, you learn about when you are touching but you are not in an embrace. When you are not in an embrace, you are in an open position. When you are in an embrace, you are in a closed position. You learn about open position first because the rules are simpler.

The Embrace

For purposes of communication, you only form an embrace on the man's right side and the woman's left side. When you are in an embrace, you are in a closed position. This is called a closed position because one side is closed by the embrace.

Open Position

> Definition of Open Position: any physically connected
> position that is not closed by the embrace.

Hands may be joined in any number of ways. Contact may also be made with other parts of the body besides the hands.

Making Connection in Open Position

The man makes the connection in open position. He either takes the woman's hands, or he connects with some other part of her body, or he presents a connection to which the woman connects.

Follow the Connection the Man Presented

In open position, the woman follows the connection the man made with her. When the man makes the connection, whatever parts are touching that is the connection. The woman maintains this connection. The woman follows those parts that are touching.

Woman's Free Hand

> I follow what I feel. What am I doing wrong? ~ Tanya, social dancer

If the woman has one or both hands free, she may touch the man but that does not form a connection for communication purposes. The woman does not maintain the connection she optionally made with her free hand. The woman does not follow what she feels with her free hand. If the man moves, away the woman must be careful not to follow after him with her free hand. When the man moves away, she must release her free hand connection.

No Hands on the Man's Arms

> It was exhausting holding her up. Now I know what you have been telling me for years. ~ Soojin, social dancer

Unless the man specifically invited the woman to do so, the woman should not place her hand on the man's arm. There is a tendency for some women to place their free hand on the man's forearm, elbow, or upper arm. This restricts the movement of the man. This is a lazy position for the woman. You must hold up your own arms.

Man's Left and Woman's Right Side

The man's left and woman's right side is the opposite side from the embrace. When the man connects with the woman by putting his left hand on her back, this is still an open position, not a closed position.

The woman does not close the position on her right side as far as that being a connection for communicating. She may put her right hand on the man's body, but she does not maintain her right hand on the man as a connection. While this may seem like an embrace, this is not an embrace for communication purposes. She still only follows the man's left hand on her back, not her right hand on the man's body.

Breaking the Connection in Open Position

The man breaks the connection in open position by moving his hands, or whatever is touching, away from the woman. The woman must not hang onto the man. The man should be able to release the connection without the woman reaching for the man as he moves away.

Releasing to Free Position

When the man lets go of the woman, so that you are no longer touching, you are in a free position. You then follow your rules for communicating in a free position.

Points to Remember

1. Definition of Open Position: any physically connected position that is not closed by the embrace.

2. In open positions, the woman follows only the connection the man makes with her.

3. The woman can touch the man with her free hand, but she does not follow what she feels with that hand.

4. The man's left side and the woman's right side do not form an embrace for communication purposes.

31. Closed Position

> Listen to your body ~ Alper Unger, Argentine tango instructor

Closed position is the most involved position, so you learn about closed position last.

Closed Position Differs From Open Position

Closed position differ from open position in some essential ways. This chapter discusses the rules governing the differences between open and closed position. These are some of the differences:

1. In closed position, the woman connects with the man's body by completing the embrace. In open position, the man makes the connection with the woman.

2. In closed position, the woman follows the body connection she made with the man. In open position, she follows the connection the man made with her.

3. In closed position, the woman releases the connection after the man releases the embrace. In open position, the man releases the connection.

The Embrace

> Definition of the Embrace: the man's right hand around the woman's left side and the woman's left hand on the man's body.

The man forms an embrace with his right arm around the woman. The woman completes the embrace with her left hand on the man's body. The essential characteristic of the embrace is the woman making a connection with the man's body. If the woman is not making a connection with the man's body, you are not in an embrace.

Closed Position

> Definition of Closed Position: the man and woman are in an embrace.

Closed position is when the man and woman connect with an embrace. The woman positions herself comfortably inside the embrace.

Closed Side

> Definition of Closed Side: the side with the embrace, the man's right side and the woman's left side.

The side with the embrace, the man's right and the woman's left, is the closed side. The woman connects with the man's body on the closed side. There is less room to maneuver on the closed side. Only this side is the closed side regardless of what type of connection is on the other side. Even if the other side seems to have the same configuration, the other side is never the closed side, unless they are dancing southpaw.

Open Side

> Definition of Open Side: the side opposite the closed side, the man's left side and the woman's right side.

The side without the embrace, the man's left and the woman's right, is the open side. There is more room to maneuver on the open side. The open side may or may not be connected. To connect on the open side, the man makes a connection with his left hand to the woman's right hand, or the man presents his left hand to which the woman connects. Various handholds are possible. Other connections on the open side are possible, such as with the man's left hand on the woman's body.

Open Embrace

Definition of Open Embrace: not in body contact.

There are two types of embrace, close embrace and open embrace. The rules for dancing in an open embrace and a close embrace are the same except for the details mentioned in this chapter. Open embrace is when you are not in body contact regardless of how close together you are. Open embrace is easier. There is more room to maneuver. There is more room for error. You can compensate for inaccuracies by adjusting the position of your arms. Open embrace is the default.

Close Embrace

Definition of Close Embrace: in body contact.

Dancing in close embrace means you are in body contact. When dancing in body contact, the woman sticks to the man like a fly on the wall. Both partners must agree to dance in body contact, otherwise you dance in an open embrace. Close embrace offers more sensitivity to your communication. Close embrace requires more skill since someone is standing up against you. There is little room to maneuver. There is little room for error. The man chooses which embrace to propose.

The Man Invites the Woman To Make Connection to Closed Position

When you embrace your partner, breath. ~ David Chayes, Argentine tango instructor

Connection in closed position is through the embrace. The man invites the woman to make a connection to a closed position. This differs from making a connection to an open position. In open position, the man makes the connection. In closed position, the woman makes the connection, after the man invites her to do so.

Closing to Open Embrace

> Rule of Closing to Open Embrace: when the man places his right hand on the woman's left shoulder blade, the woman places her right hand on the front of the man's right shoulder to complete the open embrace.

The man asks the woman to complete the open embrace by placing his right hand on the woman's left shoulder blade. The woman raises her left arm above and then down on the man's right arm, elbow outside, closing the gaps between the arms. The woman completes the open embrace by placing her left hand on the front of the man's right shoulder. Other positions of the man's and woman's hands are possible but problematic. See the Appendix topic Closed Position Open Embrace.

Closing to Close Embrace

> Rule of Closing to Close Embrace: when the man presents his frame to invite the woman to close embrace, the woman completes the embrace by positioning herself in body contact with the man.

The man invites the woman to enter a close embrace by presenting his frame to the woman. The man can invite the woman to a close embrace from an open embrace, from an open position, and from a free position. If the woman does not want to dance in body contact, she places her right hand on the front of the man's shoulder to form an open embrace. If she wants to dance in body contact, she places herself comfortably inside the man's frame connecting with her sternum on the man's body. The man's right arm and the woman's left arm go around their partner. Other close embrace positions are possible. Different dances have different needs. People have different shapes. You accommodate your close embrace to your partner.

Be Respectful of Body Parts

> Leave room for baby Jesus. ~ Neys Milo, Argentine tango professional instructor and performer

Be aware of what body part is touching what. Social dancing is not the time to cop a feel. To an outsider, watching you dance in a close embrace may look romantic. To you, the feeling should be more akin to playing tennis. Air space should remain between naughty parts.

The Man's Left Hand and the Woman's Right Hand Shape the Open Side of the Woman's Frame

The man's left hand and the woman's right hand may form another contact point at the man's option. The man uses this connection to shape the woman's frame on the open side. Do not lead with this connection in a closed position. Lead with your body. Be careful not to use pressure in this connection. You dance without the use of force.

Connection in Closed Position Is With the Man's Body

All the points that are touching are part of the connection except any optional touching made by the woman. The primary connection in closed position is the one the woman made with the man's body. This differs from open position. In open position, all the points of the connection are equal. In closed position, the primary connection with the man's body is the one the woman follows.

The Man's Right Arm Gives the Angle of the Woman

The man uses his right arm to position the angle at which the woman stands to the man. The woman stays in the man's right arm. She uses the long connection along their arms to position herself relative to the man. As the man moves his right arm, the woman adjusts her angle to maintain the connection.

The Man's Right Hand on the Woman's Back Gives the Distance

> You are holding me too tight. I cannot move. ~ Yulia, ballroom dancer

In an open embrace, the man's right hand on the woman's back gives her the distance she should be from the man. Do not hold the woman in position. The woman should stay back in the man's right hand until she can go back no further. As the woman backs into the man's right hand, the man can extend his arm to allow her to back up further.

Do Not Lead With the Right Hand or Arm

> When I was less experienced, I used to turn my hand this way and that nudging the woman where I wanted her to go. ~ Mariano, Argentine tango instructor

The man should not apply pressure with his right hand or arm on the woman's back or side. Do not push, pull, or nudge the woman to where you want her to go. If you lead with the right hand on the woman's back, you force her off-balance. Lead with your body. Allow her to move on her own. Use the body connection to set the woman in motion. Follow the woman's movement with your right hand.

Leading in Closed Position

> Rule of Leading in Closed Position: the man leads with
> the connection on his body.

In closed position, the man leads with the body connection. This is the connection made by the woman. This differs from open position where the man leads with the connection he made with his hands. In an open embrace, the primary connection is the woman's hand on the front of the man's right shoulder. In a close embrace, the primary connection is the woman's sternum on the man's body. The man moves the body connection to indicate to the woman where to move. This invites the woman to move without throwing her off-balance, allowing her to do her own dancing. Since there are multiple places of contact, the man needs to be careful not to send mixed messages. The man needs to move these other points of the connection in coordination consistent with what he wants the woman to do. He needs to make sure he is inviting her to move not coercing her into moving. When moving, the man must allow flexibility in his frame to give the woman the freedom to move on her own.

Following in Closed Position

> Rule of Following in Closed Position: the woman follows
> the connection she made with the man's body.

In closed position, the woman follows the connection she made with the man's body. In open embrace, she follows the connection of her left hand on the front of the man's right shoulder. In close embrace, she follows the connection of her sternum on the man's body. While there are multiple connection points, the woman can only focus on one, which is the body connection. She still follows the law of connection to maintain all the points of the connection. She still follows her rule to maintain her frame, if possible, when the connection moves horizontally. The man depends on her following these rules to get her to move where he wants.

Releasing From Closed Position

> Rule of Releasing from Closed Position: the woman releases her body connection when the man breaks the embrace.

When the man breaks the embrace, the woman releases her body connection with the man. There are two ways the man breaks the embrace. The first is to remove his right hand from around the woman. The second is to break the body contact, either by sending the woman out of or by removing himself from the body connection. The man can use either method to release from an open embrace. The man can use only the second method, breaking the body connection, to release from a close embrace. To break the body connection, the man must cause the woman's part and the man's part of the body connection to move apart from each other. When the woman's part and the man's part move in different ways, the woman releases the body connection. When the woman's part and the man's part move together, the woman keeps the body connection.

Practice When To Make and Break From Closed Position

Unlike open position, closing to and releasing from closed position is not intuitive. You have to tell the woman how to close the position. You have to tell her how to release from closed position. You have to practice so she learns to release automatically.

Hold Up Your Own Weight

When you dance in a closed position, you must hold up your own weight. You must be careful not to use your hands or arms on your partner to hold yourself up. Besides the dangers, pressure in the hands or arms causes false signals. You must dance without pressure in the hands or arms.

Points To Remember

1. Definition of the Embrace: the man's right hand around the woman's left side and the woman's left hand on the man's body.

2. Definition of Closed Position: the man and woman are in an embrace.

3. Definition of Closed Side: the side with the embrace, the man's right side and the woman's left side.

4. Definition of Open Side: the side opposite the closed side, the man's left side and the woman's right side.

5. Definition of Open Embrace: not in body contact.

6. Definition of Close Embrace: in body contact.

7. Rule of Closing to Open Embrace: when the man places his right hand on the woman's left shoulder blade, the woman places her left hand on the front of the man's right shoulder to complete the open embrace.

8. Rule of Closing to Close Embrace: when the man presents his frame to invite the woman to close embrace, the woman completes the embrace by positioning herself in body contact with the man.

9. The man's right arm gives the angle of the woman.

10. The man's right hand on the woman's back gives the distance in open embrace.

11. Rule of Leading in Closed Position: the man leads with the connection on his body.

12. Rule of Following in Closed Position: the woman follows the connection she made with the man's body.

13. Rule of Releasing from Closed Position: the woman releases her body connection when the man breaks the embrace.

14. Hold up your own weight, do not use your hands or arms on your partner to hold yourself up.

How To Dance With a Partner

* * *

Part D for Direction

32. Direction

> The second law of Newtonian lindy hop is momentum: a follower set in motion will continue to stay in motion until that motion is changed by the lead. ~ Joel Plys, professional swing dance instructor and performer

In the last part C for Connection, you learned how to initiate the woman's movement. In this part D for Direction, you learn how the woman completes her movement. With these pieces, you can communicate every step in every dance.

The Man Invites the Woman To Move

> How do I guide the woman after I send her out? ~ Wayne, beginning swing dancer

The man does not guide the woman. The man invites the woman to move. Once he has invited her to move, he no longer leads her.

The Woman Does Her Own Dancing

Once the woman starts moving, she continues to move on her own following the rules in this part. The woman does her own dancing without further direction from the man.

Points To Remember

1. The man invites the woman to move.

2. The woman does her own dancing.

33. Law of Direction

> How do I know when to stop? ~ Vasanthi, beginning
> Argentine tango dancer

Once the woman is in motion, what happens next? She keeps going.

The Law of Direction

The Law of Direction: the woman maintains her
direction.

Once the man asks the woman to move in a particular direction, she
continues to move in that same direction until she can go no further.

Three Directions

Rule of Directions: the three directions are straight,
turn, and circle.

There are three directions the man signals the woman to go. The
three directions are:

1. Straight

2. Turn

3. Circle

Signaling the Three Directions

There are only two movements the woman can do: step and rotate.
These two movements correspond to the first two directions. When
the man wants the woman to go straight, he invites her to step. When
the man wants the woman to turn, he invites her to rotate. When the
man wants the woman to circle, he starts her walking around in a

circle. You will learn more about circling later. For now, consider circling as a variation on going straight. For a discussion on the circle direction, see the Appendix topic Circle Direction.

The Man Initiates the Woman's Movement

The man sets the woman in motion by moving the connection horizontally so that she starts to step or starts to rotate. Once the woman is in motion, the man does not do anything to her. He does not push or pull her to keep her stepping. He does not stir the pot to keep her rotating.

The Woman Continues Her Movement on Her Own

The woman continues her movement without waiting for the man to do anything else. She continues to step in a straight line, or she continues to rotate, or she continues to walk around in a circle on her own.

Connection Comes Before Direction

The law of connection comes before the law of direction. The woman maintaining the connection takes precedence over the woman maintaining her direction. The woman moves in the direction indicated as long as she can continue to maintain the connection.

Frame to Spaghetti Arms

When the man moves the connection horizontally, the woman maintains her frame to get the signal of whether to step or to rotate. Once the woman gets the signal, she goes from frame to spaghetti arms. She lets her frame adjust to her movement. She continues her movement in the direction indicated, relaxing her frame to allow her to move as far as she comfortably can.

The Man Can Alter the Connection

The man can alter the connection even while the woman is moving. He may change the connection to allow the woman to move further or to cut the woman's movement short. He can change the handhold. He can move the connection up and down. He can adjust the connection however he likes.

The Woman Cannot Alter the Connection

The woman's job is to maintain the connection. She lets the connection adjust to her movement. She does not adjust the connection to allow herself to move further.

The Woman Stops When She Can Go No Further

> Rule of Woman Stopping: the woman stops when her motion is blocked or she reaches the end of her connection.

The woman stops her movement when she can go no further. She can go no further when her motion is blocked in the direction she is going or when she reaches the end of the connection.

Blocking the Woman's Movement

To block horizontal movement, the man blocks the woman in the horizontal direction of her movement. The man blocks the woman with any part of his body blocking any part of her body in the direction she is going. When physically connected, the man blocks the woman with a physical connection. He can block her with something as small as his finger on the edge of her hand.

End of Connection

The woman stops when she reaches the end of the connection. The end of the connection is the point where the woman can go no further while still maintaining the connection.

The Man Does Not Stop the Woman

The man could hurt the woman if he attempted to stop her. Everyone moves on their own. Everyone stops on their own.

How Does the Man Let the Woman Know Where to Stop?

The man positions the connection to indicate where the woman stops. To block the woman, the man positions some part of the connection in the woman's way in the direction she is going. Alternatively, the man positions the connection at the point where she can go no further.

The Woman Is Free To Dance However She Likes

> When the woman wants to hijack the lead, she puts her hand on the man's wrist. This lets the man know to stop leading. ~ West Coast swing dance instructor

There is no need for the woman to give the man an indication that she may deviate from basic steps. Once the woman is in motion, the woman is free to dance however she wants as long as she follows the laws of balance, connection, and direction. She can do whatever steps she chooses. She can take as much or as little time as she likes to complete her movement. See the Appendix topic Dance As If for a discussion on the topic of following the rules.

The Man Waits for the Woman To Finish

Once the man sets the woman moving, the man waits for the woman to finish. When the woman is done the man invites the woman to do something else.

The Man Is Free To Move on His Own

Once the man sets the woman in motion, the man is free to move on his own. Since the man does not guide the woman through her steps, he can move in any way that is available to him. The man knows where the woman is going. He can meet her at any point he chooses. He is not constrained by having to hang onto her. He has the maximum freedom to express himself.

Points To Remember

1. Law of Direction: the woman maintains her direction.

2. Rule of Directions: the three directions are straight, turn, and circle.

3. The woman continues her movement on her own.

4. Rule of Woman Stopping: the woman stops when her motion is blocked or she reaches the end of her connection.

5. The woman is free to dance however she likes.

6. The man waits for the woman to finish.

34. Basic Patterns

> Figures are simple. All the lady does is go straight and turn around. ~ Eduardo, salsa instructor

All the choreography for the woman is made up of four basic patterns. The four basic patterns follow logically from the law of direction.

Four Basic Patterns

> "We use five 6-count figures as a teaching tool," I said.
>
> "I see," said Chris, a beginning swing dancer. "We learn the figures to make up the dance."
>
> "No," I answered. "You lead and follow signals. The figures are for practicing the signals."

The man initiates the woman's movement by sending her a signal. He sends her the signal by moving the connection horizontally. He invites her to step, rotate, or circle. Once the woman is in motion, she keeps going until she can go no further. Logically, this implies there are four basic patterns for the woman:

1. Go straight

2. Turn in place

3. Walk around in a circle

4. Turn while traveling

Go Straight Basic Pattern

The first basic pattern is to go straight. Asking the woman to step in a specific direction is the signal to go straight in that direction. The woman is to continue to go straight in that direction until she can go no further. She ends facing the same direction she started.

Turn in Place Basic Pattern

The second basic pattern is to turn in place. Asking the woman to rotate while she is in place is the turn in place signal. The woman is to continue turning in place until she can turn no further. When she finishes her turn, she should be in the same place she started. She may be facing a different direction depending on where the man invited her to stop.

Walk Around in a Circle Basic Pattern

> I was watching a professional dancer leading his partner to walk around him in a circle. He pulled her around him with one hand. With the other hand, he awkwardly reached behind her to nudge her around.

The third basic pattern is for the woman to walk in a circular pattern either around her partner or away from and back to her partner. To signal the woman to walk in a circle, the man starts the woman walking in a circle. The woman continues the circular pattern until stopped. The walk around in a circle pattern is the equivalent of the go straight pattern. Rules that apply to going straight apply to walking around in a circle.

Turn While Traveling Basic Pattern

The fourth basic pattern is to turn while traveling. Turn while traveling is part of going straight and circling. First, the man initiates the woman's movement to go straight or walk around in a circle. When the woman begins her movement, she is traveling along a line or circle. Once the woman has started to travel, the man may invite the woman to add a traveling turn. The woman turns while continuing to go straight or circling. After the woman completes her traveling turn, she then completes going straight or circling in her original direction regardless of the direction she is facing.

First, the man stops the woman's turn, then he stops the woman from going straight or circling. The man may stop the woman's turn in one direction then invite her to turn in the opposite direction. This may be repeated multiple times. When the woman finishes all her turns, she finishes going straight.

Points To Remember

1. The four basic patterns are go straight, turn in place, walk around in a circle, and turn while traveling.

2. When the man invites the woman to step, the woman goes straight.

3. When the man invites the woman to rotate while the woman is standing in place, the woman turns in place.

4. When the man invites the woman to walk around in a circle, the woman travels in a circle either around the man or away from and back to the man.

5. Once the woman has begun to go straight or circle, when the man invites the woman to rotate, the woman turns while continuing to travel. After completing her turn, she completes going straight or circling.

35. Woman's Choreography

> Like everything in life, I will get started and everything
> will work out. ~ Kay, social dancer

Essentially, all the man asks the woman to do is go straight and turn. Next time you are out dancing, watch the woman. No matter how complex the figure, all her choreography can be broken down into these two movements. The one exception is to walk around in a circle. Consider walking around in a circle as a variation of going straight.

Vertical Movement, Handholds, and the Man's Choreography

You can think of vertical movement, different handholds, and the man's choreography as embellishments. They are not relevant to understanding the woman's horizontal movement.

Building Blocks for Figures

The four basic patterns are the building blocks for the woman's figures. The woman's figures are made up these basic patterns following one upon another.

The Unit of Communication

> Definition of the Unit of Communication: the man invites the woman to move. The woman completes her movement. The man waits for her to finish.

As you dance, there is a parade of requests that the man makes of the woman. The man invites the woman then waits for her to finish. The woman completes her movement on her own. This sequence of invitation by the man and completion by the woman is the unit of communication.

Communicating the Woman's Choreography via Basic Patterns

To lead and follow a woman's figure, you lead and follow the basic patterns that make up the figure. Break the figure into the basic patterns. Communicate the basic patterns, not the figure.

Woman's Line of Dance

> Definition of the Woman's Line of Dance: the line on which the woman dances.

When the woman begins to go straight, the direction in which the woman starts to step establishes her line of dance. Once established, the woman's line of dance stays the same regardless of where the man moves. The woman continues with every step on her line until her movement is stopped in that direction. Her next line of dance may be in any direction. When the woman is circling, the woman's line of dance is a circle.

Dancing on a Railroad Track

Think of the woman's line of dance as a railroad track. The woman dances in the center. The man dances on the rails. The man may move on and off the woman's line of dance. When he wants her to stop, he stays in her way, blocking her movement. When he wants her to pass, he gets out of her way.

Stay on Your Line

For the woman, take every step on your line of dance. You own your line. If the man is in your way, stop. Do not go around the man. Glare at him until he moves out of the way.

Half Turn per Step

For the woman, when you turn while traveling, you take every step, even your turning steps, on your line of dance. You make half a turn with each step. First you step, then you turn halfway. You should not step and turn at the same time, otherwise, you will be like a wobbly top.

Finish Going Straight

For the woman, after you finish turning, regardless of the direction you are facing, finish stepping down your line of dance in your original direction.

Straight, Turn, Finish Going Straight

> I am confused. I do not know where to go. ~ Jana, beginning social dancer

For the woman, the answer to many questions you have is to go straight, turn, finishing going straight. This is the simple formula for much of the woman's choreography. When you are confused about where to go, remember to go straight, turn if requested, then finish going straight in your original direction.

Where the Man Goes Has Nothing to Do With You

If the man signals you to move, you move where signaled. If the man does not signal you to move, stay where you are. Do not adjust your position to where the man is unless he signals you to do so.

The Communication to the Woman Is Simple

The man can communicate the woman's choreography because what the woman is to do is defined by the simple set of rules described in this book. This simplicity allows unambiguous communication. This simplicity allows the man to lead and the woman to follow.

Communicating the Man's Choreography Is Not Possible

While the woman is doing something simple, the man may make a number of movements too complex to describe in a simple communication system. No matter how experienced a dancer she is, the woman cannot lead all the man's steps while she is dancing the woman's role.

Points To Remember

1. Essentially, all the man asks the woman to do is go straight and turn.

2. Vertical movement, handholds, and the man's choreography are not relevant to understanding the woman's horizontal movement.

3. Definition of the Unit of Communication: the man invites the woman to move. The woman completes her movement. The man waits for her to finish.

4. Definition of the Woman's Line of Dance: the line on which the woman dances.

5. For the women, stay on your line.

6. Once the woman is in motion going straight or circling, the man may ask the woman to add a turn.

7. When turning while traveling, the woman makes a half turn on each step.

Part D for Direction

8. The simple formula for much of the woman's choreography is to go straight, turn, finish going straight.

9. The man can communicate all the woman's choreography, but the woman cannot communicate all the man's choreography.

36. Moving With Your Partner

The leader owns the follower's free leg. ~ Andrea Pham, Argentine tango instructor

The Man Is Responsible for the Woman's Free Foot

Rule of Woman's Free Foot: the man is responsible for the woman's free foot.

The man is responsible for the woman being on the correct foot. The man is responsible for knowing where the woman's weight is. If the man does not know which foot the woman is standing on, he needs to adjust the connection until he knows which foot the woman is prepared to move.

Stand on One Foot or the Other

Which foot do I step with next? ~ Chris, social dancer

The woman should be on one foot or the other. She should not stand on both feet unless the man put her there. She should have one foot free to move.

Do Not Change Weight on Your Own

I was dancing Argentine tango with a woman. I switched feet to cross-system. I started to step inside the foot she was standing on. She thought she was on the wrong foot. While I was in mid-stride, she quickly switched her feet. I stepped right into her toe. Ouch. The result was not pretty.

If the woman suspects she is on the wrong foot, she should not change weight in the middle of her movement to her other foot on her own. She should let the man change her weight. If the woman suddenly changes weight on her own, she is liable to get stepped on. The man initiates a movement expecting the woman to step with her free foot. If the woman unexpectedly changes her feet, the man may step into the space he expects to be free which instead is occupied by the woman's changed foot. You can get hurt that way.

Do Not Lead Until You Know Which Foot Is Free

> Paul kept stepping on Linda at a specific place. I tried leading Linda. She was fine. I tried following Paul. He was a good leader, but had the same problem with me. When he brought his feet together, he changed his weight but did not change his partner's weight.

When you lead, you must know which foot the woman has free. Do not step until you are sure. If you are not sure, get sure. Adjust the position to make sure the woman will step with the appropriate foot.

Be Clear

Be clear about where you are so your partner knows what to do. Be clear about which foot you are standing on. Be clear about where you are going.

Do Not Let Your Partner Step on Your Foot

> Rule of Stepping Backward: whoever is moving backward is responsible for not getting their foot stepped on.

If you are moving backward, you are responsible for not letting your partner step on your foot, at least not the foot you are stepping with. The most certain way not to get stepped on is to wait for your partner to put their foot down first. After your partner steps, then you step.

Do Not Let Your Partner Bump Knees With You

> I was dancing Argentine tango when Emily complained, "We keep bumping knees." Some months later, Pipi complained about the same thing.

If you are moving backward, do not let your partner bump knees with you either. When your partner starts to come forward, get your leg out of the way. Do not just bend your knee. Move your thigh out of the way too. Make space for your partner to step into.

Points To Remember

1. Rule of Woman's Free Foot: the man is responsible for the woman's free foot.

2. The woman should be on one foot, not both.

3. The woman should not change weight on her own.

4. Be clear.

5. Rule of Stepping Backward: whoever is moving backward is responsible for not getting their foot stepped on.

37. Following Visually

> Jonathan King, contra dance caller: "Why aren't you dancing?"
>
> Sitting Man: "I have two left feet."
>
> Jonathan: "I know a dance choreographed especially for men with two left feet. It is a partner dance. The woman's part is for a woman with two right feet."

When the man and woman are not physically connected, the woman follows visually. The woman follows as if they were connected physically at a distance. The same rules you have learned continue to apply except the connection is visual. Here are the highlights on leading and following visually.

Establishing a Visual Connection

The man establishes a visual connection with the woman in some obvious way. The man positions himself in some way that the woman can see that he is starting a visual connection.

The Connection Is in the Middle

When following visually the connection point is in the middle. The woman adjusts her position according to the middle point between the man and the woman. If the man is moving in the opposite direction of the woman, the woman moves away from or to the middle point as the man does the same. If they are moving in the same direction, the woman keeps the middle point at the same distance from each other.

Follow Visually by Mirroring

Rule of Mirroring: when not physically connected, the woman follows by mirroring the man.

The woman visually follows every step of the man by mirroring him. The woman follows by making the same relative movements, taking into consideration the foot she starts on and the direction she is going at the time of visual connection. The woman may be on the same or opposite foot of the man. She may be going in the same or opposite direction.

Continuing Her Motion

When following visually, there are times when the woman loses sight of the man. Typically this happens during a turn. The woman should continue in whatever motion she is going, such as turning. When she regains sight of the man, the man may have repositioned himself. The woman should not reposition herself. In this case, the couple establishes a new visual connection from the new position.

Points To Remember

1. The man establishes a visual connection with a woman by aligning himself with the woman in some obvious way.

2. The connection is in the middle.

3. Rule of Mirroring: when not physically connected, the woman follows as if physically connected, by mirroring.

How To Dance With a Partner

* * *

Part Skill

38. Balance Skills

> To teach steps is easy. To teach balance is difficult. ~ Andrei, Argentine tango instructor

You now return to the subject of balance. In this part, you learn physical skills for communicating with your partner.

You Learned What To Do

Until now, you learned the rules for dancing with a partner. You learned the language of communicating in social dancing. You learned that everyone maintains their own balance which means no pushing and pulling. You learned the man's responsibilities are to position the couple on the dance floor, keep time with the music, and initiate the choreography. You learned the woman's responsibilities are to keep time with the man, maintain the connection, and complete her movement. You learned the woman maintains her frame when the man moves the connection horizontally, otherwise, she lets her frame adjust. You learned there are two movements when standing on one leg, step and rotate. You learned you use the two movements to initiate the four basic patterns of go straight, turn in place, circle, and turn while traveling. You learned once the woman is in motion, she is to continue in the same motion. You learned the woman stops when her movement is blocked or she reaches the end of her connection. You learned the man waits for the woman to finish.

You Learn How To Move

There is one more thing you need to learn to communicate with your partner. Now that you know what to do, you need to learn how to move to do what you learned. How you move is sometimes called technique. Technique is best addressed by your dance teacher in person where they can give you personal feedback. You need to experience how to move. You need to practice moving effectively.

You need to train yourself through appropriate exercises. Good exercises train your body to automatically move in the way you want. You need to dance a lot so that your body learns how to move with your partner. There is no substitute for DT, dance time.

The Rules Are Logically Complete

The rules you have learned are a procedural system for dancing with a partner. They are a mathematical formula of sorts. The rules are logically complete, presumably. They are all the communication rules you need to dance with a partner socially. If you break the rules, you suffer consequences which are a loss of one or more of the ten values under attitude. For example, if the woman breaks the connection, she will not know what the man is asking her to do. If the woman does not stay on her line of dance, the man will not know where the woman is going. In these cases, the communication will be ambiguous.

Technique Is What Works

> In basketball, the rule is you have to put the ball in the basket to score points. The rules do not tell you how you put the ball in the basket. Putting the ball in the basket is a skill.

Technique is different from the rules. Technique is about what works. Technique is how you move. Technique is the physical skill that allows you to accomplish your objective. In this part, you learn skills for dancing with a partner. People come in different shapes, sizes, and abilities. While one set of communication rules works for everyone, physical techniques for implementing those skills may vary. The suggestions under these balance skills work in many circumstances. You may find that some of these suggestions do not work for you at times. You certainly will find additional techniques not mentioned here. If you figure out something that works, as long as the technique does not violate the rules, your technique is a good one. The rules take precedence over technique.

Points To Remember

1. In this part, you learn physical skills to communicate with a partner.

2. Any technique is good if the technique works as long as you do not violate the rules.

39. Move as One

> Take time to connect with your partner before you start dancing. ~ David Chayes, Argentine tango instructor

Moving as One

The objective is for two people to move as one, one body with four legs and all that. Keep this in your mind as you dance.

Wait To Move With Your Partner

To move with your partner, wait for your partner to move. Then move with your partner, coordinating your movement to your partner's movement. Time your steps with your partner's steps. Time your weight changes with your partner's weight changes.

Use Your Frame as a Shock Absorber

When your partner moves, you should not immediately move your body. Allow your frame to soften. You use your hands and arms to act as a shock absorber to give you some time to respond to your partner. This shock-absorbing action may not be visibly noticeable. You still need to maintain your frame. Your frame should give as much as necessary then bounce back to shape.

The Feet Are for Moving the Body

Dancing is done with the body. The feet are for moving the body. When you step, think about moving your body not your foot. Your partner cannot feel your feet. Your partner is connected to your body through your frame. Move your body to communicate with your partner effectively.

Do Not Push Your Head Forward

> When losing connection with my partner, I found myself
> leaning forward to stay closer. This made things worse.
> As my head came forward, my body went back.

People tend to move from their head. They feel they are where their
head is at. When you lose contact with your partner, to reconnect,
you may push your head forward. Pushing your head forward pushes
your body back exacerbating your loss of connection. When you lose
connection, keep your head back so your body stays forward. Lead
your movement from your body, not your head.

Step Into Your Partner

When stepping forward into your partner, step into the space your
partner is vacating. Place your free foot next to your partner's
supporting foot underneath your partner's body. This keeps you
together moving smoothly without causing each other to wobble.

Move Forward With Conviction

Move forward with power in your body. Even though there is a
person, your partner, standing where you want to step, step into the
space with confidence. Your partner is moving out of the way.

Do Not Dodge Your Partner

If your partner is in your way, stop. Do not go out of your way to go
around your partner. Wait for your partner to pass, then move into
the space. When you dodge your partner, you go away from your
partner, putting you in an awkward position.

Eight Directions To Step, Two Directions To Turn

There are eight directions in which you can step without changing your forward-facing direction. You can step forward, back, both sides, and the four diagonals. You can also turn to change your facing direction. You can turn to your left or right.

Disassociation

When you step straight forward, back, or to either side, while your body is facing forward, your torso and hips stay in the same alignment. When you step on a diagonal while your body is facing forward, you become something of a contortionist. Your torso stays facing forward while your hips turn towards the direction you are stepping. Your legs may have to turn even further than your hips. The separation of movement between your upper and lower body is called disassociation.

Disassociate To Maintain Connection

When dancing with a partner, you disassociate to maintain the connection and your frame. The woman disassociates according to the laws of connection and direction. The man disassociates as needed to communicate with his partner.

Points To Remember

1. Move as one.

2. Wait to move with your partner.

3. Use your frame as a shock absorber.

4. The feet are for moving the body.

5. Disassociate to maintain the connection.

40. Taking a Step on Your Own

> Finish your step so I can finish mine. ~ Thuy Carrol, Argentine tango instructor

To move well with your partner, you must first learn to move well on your own. A comprehensive explanation of how to move is impossible. Still, without knowing how to move, how can you dance?

Build Your Foundation One Skill at a Time

> When I took up dancing in body contact in Argentine tango, I was unable to take a single step. Tango exposed how bad my body mechanics were.

How to move is an issue best addressed in person by your dance teachers for the particular dance that you are doing. Here are guidelines, not rules, to raise your body awareness. Some may seem contradictory. Use these guidelines as appropriate. Work on the guidelines in the order presented. The guidelines build upon one another. Build your foundation one skill at a time.

Do Not Stand on Two Feet, Stand on One Foot or the Other

Like most people, you are probably used to standing on two feet. The problem is when you stand on two feet you cannot move. You must first shift your weight to one foot so you can take a step with the other foot. When you dance, when you bring your feet together, have your weight on one foot or the other, not both.

Stand on the Sturdy Part of Your Foot

> My feet were cramping. I think I was dancing too far forward on my toes. ~ Kellyann, social dancer

Stand on the sturdy part of your foot. Standing on the sturdy part of your foot gives you the most stability. This allows you to move your weight a small amount forward or backward without committing to a step. Being able to move a small amount is useful for communicating. Standing on the sturdy part of your foot gives you the most control over your step. This allows you to stay balanced throughout your movement.

Feet Together Underneath the Body

Stand with your feet together underneath your body, not underneath your hips. You need to have your feet underneath your body, in the center, so you can balance on one foot.

Do Not Walk With Your Feet Under Your Hips

While dance teachers say if you can walk you can dance, which is true, walking is not dancing. People naturally walk like ducks. People waddle when they walk. Your legs are under your hips. Your body is centered between your legs. If you walk with some space between your feet, you are walking on two lines, one for each foot. Your body sways from side to side, like a duck. Waddling to music with your partner is not easy.

Walk on a Line

For better balance, walk on a line. Imagine a line on the floor. When you walk, place your foot on the line. You do not have to place the center part of your foot on the line. As long as some part of your foot is on the line, you are fine. Walking on a line keeps your feet underneath the center of your body, eliminating waddling. Your head and body remain steady. Practice walking on a line going forward and backward.

Move From Your Center

Think about moving your body, rather than moving your foot or your head.

Use Your Behind

Use the muscles in your hips to move your body. Power your movement with these big muscles. Use these muscles to push in the direction you are stepping. Use these muscles to pull your leg to your body.

Soften Your Knees

Do not lock your knees. Soften the knee of your supporting leg with a little bend. This allows you to balance over the sturdy part of your foot while you move. Do not lift your knee up, as that will cause you to prance unless prancing is what you want to do.

Straight Legs

Try to straighten your legs to give you a consistent stride. Straightening your legs can help keep you from bouncing.

Brush the Floor

Brush the floor with your free foot as you move. The sensation of touch gives you better balance. You do not use your free foot to support your weight while moving.

Reach With Your Free Foot

Before stepping, reach with your free foot. Position your free foot securely on the floor.

Push Off the Floor

When you move, think about pushing the floor with your supporting leg. This keeps your weight on your supporting leg instead of falling onto your free foot. This gives you better balance while you step.

Transfer Your Weight

Transfer your weight from your supporting leg to your free leg. Stay balanced as you transfer your weight. Control your movement all the way through your step. Avoid falling from one foot to the other.

Bring Your Knees and Ankles Together

When you finish one step to start another, bring your knees and ankles together. This keeps you balanced on one leg as your body passes over your foot. You walk more smoothly, allowing you to walk more easily with your partner. By being balanced, you can stop right where you are, standing on one leg.

Collect Your Feet

Bring your new free foot, with knees and ankles together, up to your new supporting leg. This helps to bring your body over your foot.

Finish With Your Weight Fully Over Your Foot

Move your body all the way over your foot. When you are done with your step, you should have no weight on your starting foot.

Balance Over Each Complete Step

Balance over every complete step as you move. Being balanced on one leg allows you to stop where you are, move smoothly, change directions, and alter timing. Be free to step in any direction after you finish each step.

One Step at a Time

Take one step at a time. Follow the procedure for each step from start to finish. Do not rush to the next step. Avoid letting your momentum carry you from one step to another. Control your movement.

Walk Over the Middle, Front, and Back of Your Stride

As you practice walking on a line, walk so that your body is in the middle of your stride. Middle meaning from front to back, so that your body is between your front foot and back foot, staying close to the middle between the two. Then move your body forward, so that you are walking over your front foot. Lastly move your body back, so that you are walking over your back foot. Being able to walk in all positions is useful.

Contra Body Movement

Contra body movement takes place when your upper body turns toward your forward foot. When you step forward with your right foot, the left side of your chest comes forward, while the right side of your chest goes back. Contra body movement is useful. To practice contra body movement, practice walking on a line. Instead of stepping on the line, reach across the line with your foot. With your next step, reach across to the other side of the line. You are crossing over the line as you take each step. Keep your body facing straight ahead. This gives you the contra body movement because you have to turn your upper body into your forward leg. Try the same exercise backward.

Remember the Principle of Naturalness

Keep in mind the principle of naturalness. Your movements should be natural to the human body. They may not be comfortable for you yet, but you should see them as being natural to you once you get used to them. If your interpretation of anything you read here is unnatural, rethink what you are doing. As you retrain your body to move this way, you should look more like a dancer. While good looks do not always reflect natural movement, natural movement should result in smoother looks.

Points To Remember

1. Stand on one foot or the other.

2. Stand on the sturdy part of your foot.

3. Feet together underneath the body.

4. Walk on a line.

5. Move from your center.

6. Use your behind.

7. Soften your knees.

8. Straight legs.

9. Brush the floor.

10. Reach with your free foot.

11. Push off the floor.

12. Transfer Your Weight.

13. Bring your knees and ankles together.

14. Collect your feet.

15. Finish with your weight fully over your foot.

16. Balance over each complete step.

17. Take one step at a time.

18. Be natural.

41. Transfer Your Weight

> Reach with your front foot. Use your back foot to help
> you step. ~ David Chayes, Argentine tango instructor

People naturally walk by falling from one step to the next. This is an efficient way to walk. People doing the March of Dimes marathon can walk 20 miles in a day without training. While this is a good way to walk, if you fall towards each step while you dance, you are going to have problems. You are not balanced throughout your step. You have committed your body to move to your next step regardless of what your partner is doing. You cannot control your movement. You are unable to respond to your partner while you step. You cannot stop while you are stepping.

You Must Be Balanced While You Step

To be able to lead and follow every step, you must be able to control your step. You must be balanced while you step to coordinate your timing and position.

Transfer Your Weight

To control your step, you must learn to transfer your. The guidelines here are an emphasis of the previous chapter Taking a Step. You learn how to take a step by transferring your weight without falling from one foot to the other.

Move Like a Cat

> Cats balance on three legs while moving their free foot.
> After placing their free foot, cats shift weight to balance
> on three other legs before moving another foot. Rock
> climbing humans do the same thing. Rock climbers
> secure three limbs while moving their fourth. Once the

fourth limb is secure, rock climbers shift their weight to a new secure position. At no point are the rock climbers off-balance.

When you dance, move like a cat or a rock climber. With your supporting leg secure, place your free foot.

Dance Like a Ninja

Think of a ninja dancing on rice paper. The ninja balances with all their weight on one foot, while they softly place the other foot so as not to move the rice paper. The ninja then carefully transfers their weight from one foot to the other, remaining balanced the whole time so that the rice paper does not tear.

Human dancers move on two legs, not four. Dance like a ninja. Transfer your weight with control from your supporting foot to your free foot.

Empty Step

When you reach with one foot, while you have all your weight on your other foot, Qigong practitioners call this an empty step. An empty step is when you have your free foot in position for the next step, but you have no weight on that foot.

Before transferring your weight, you can tap the floor with your free foot in place. During your weight transfer, you have your weight on both feet. You increase your weight on your newly placed foot. You decrease your weight on your initial supporting leg until the weight on your initial supporting leg goes to zero. At that point, you have all your weight on your newly placed foot. You have no weight on your prior supporting leg. You can tap the ground with your new free foot. Throughout this process, your body is balanced. At no time do you fall from one foot to the other. Though the posture for dancing differs from that of Qigong, the principle of the empty step is the same.

Keep Your Weight on Your Supporting Leg

When moving, keep your weight on your supporting leg so you are in control throughout the entire length of your stride. Bend the knee of your supporting leg to lengthen your stride.

Keep Your Body Over Your Supporting Leg

As you reach with your free foot, keep your body over your supporting leg. When you go forward, keep your body over your back foot. When you go backward, keep your body over your front foot.

Place Your Free Foot

Place your free foot rather than plopping your foot down. When practicing slowly, tap the floor before placing your foot. This is your empty step position at the beginning.

Push Off Your Supporting Foot

Push off your supporting foot to move your body to the foot you just placed. Shift your weight smoothly to that foot.

Release Your Initial Supporting Foot

When your weight is fully transferred, you should have no weight on your initial supporting leg. Your initial supporting foot should still be in your starting position. When practicing slowly, tap the floor with this foot before collecting your feet. This is your empty step position at the end.

Practice Transferring Weight While Walking on a Line

Practice transferring your weight while walking on a line as described in the prior section on Taking a Step. First, practice walking on a line. Next, practice crossing over the line for contra body movement. Add practicing transferring your weight as you step. Imagine yourself moving on rice paper. Place your foot. Tap the floor in empty step position. Go slow, as if you were in slow motion. Transfer your weight. Make sure you are able to stop at any point.

The Ninja H

You can practice transferring your weight any time you are standing up. You do not need to have room to walk. Start with your weight on your left foot with your feet together. Reach with your right foot to the side. Tap your right foot to make sure you have no weight on your free foot. Place your free foot. Push with your left foot to transfer your weight to your right foot. Pull with your right leg. Be able to stop at any point between your feet. Fully transfer your weight. Tap with your left foot to make sure you have no weight on your starting foot. Bring your knees, ankles, and feet together. Repeat your sidestep to the left. Vary the length of your sidestep. Sometimes, transfer your weight without moving your foot so you are transferring your weight in place, which is a tiny sidestep. Do the same thing forward and back on both sides, so you form the shape of an H. Take one or more steps forward and back. Use contra body movement on your steps, forward, back, and side.

Points To Remember

1. Transfer your weight.

2. Move like a cat.

3. Dance like a ninja.

4. Push off your supporting leg, pull with your newly placed leg.

5. Practice the ninja H.

42. Rhythm

Dancing will change your life. ~ David, salsa instructor

Many social dances have a basic rhythm to which you dance. The rhythm is the timing of steps you take to a particular number of beats of music.

The Woman Keeps Time With the Man

Ladies, do not try to help the man keep time with the music. Try to enjoy his unique, musical interpretation.

The woman keeps time with the man, not the music. If the man is not keeping the beat, the woman still must keep time with the man. This is the only way you can dance together.

Synchronize To Get Started

At the start of a dance, the first thing you should do is to synchronize with your partner. The man should position the connection so that the woman must stand on a particular foot. Once the woman is in position ready to dance, the man can initiate movement. During the dance, when getting out of time with your partner, the man can resynchronize with this same procedure.

Movement of the Connection Indicates the Rhythm

The man communicates rhythm by how he moves the connection. The woman should pay attention to the connection to get her timing. She should not try to look at the man's feet to figure out what to do.

Rhythm Changes

The simplest rhythm is when you take a step to one beat of the music, like marching. To change the rhythm you can take away steps by pausing on a beat of the music or you can add steps in between beats of the music. Signaling and following rhythm changes provide a challenge that tests your skill.

Use Complete and Partial Steps

One way to communicating rhythm changes is the man either asking the woman to take a complete step or a partial step. When the woman takes a complete step, she is balanced over her supporting leg. A complete step takes more time. To lead a woman to a complete step, the man moves the connection so that the woman moves her body over her supporting leg. After a complete step, she is able to pause.

When the woman takes a partial step, she does not move her body over her new supporting leg. At the end of her partial step, she is not balanced over her supporting leg. She must move back to her other foot. To lead a woman to a partial step, the man moves the connection so that the woman only moves partway to her supporting leg. He then moves the connection to lead her to her next step. In this manner, he can lead the woman to quicker steps.

Focus on Balance, Connection, and Posture

The woman should not try to do the steps the man is leading. Following rhythm changes is too fast for thinking. The woman should focus on balance. She should pay attention to maintaining the connection. She should maintain her posture. She should try to transfer her weight. She should attempt to complete her step, stopping appropriately. In this way, her steps, even fast ones, will come automatically.

42. Rhythm

Points To Remember

1. Rhythm changes are adding or taking away steps.

2. The woman keeps time with the man.

3. Synchronize to get started.

4. The movement of the connection indicates the rhythm.

5. Use complete steps and partial steps to signal rhythm changes.

6. The woman should focus on balance, connection, and posture to do her steps automatically.

43. Turning

> You have to stop your forward momentum before you turn. ~ Jorge Torres, professional Argentine tango performer and instructor

Here are some things to be aware of when you turn. If you are struggling in a particular turn, see if any of these help.

Maintain Your Posture While Turning

Maintain your posture while you turn. When you turn, you are rotating around your supporting leg. To be balanced while you turn, your posture needs to be straight up and down.

Do Not Bend Over While Turning

To get under your partner's arm, if you need to, you can lower yourself by bending your knees, keeping your head straight up. Do not bend over. If you bend over while you turn, your turn will be out of control.

Do Not Turn and Step at the Same Time

For the best balance, your posture should be stable. Step before or after you turn. Avoid turning and stepping at the same time. If you turn while stepping, you are likely to take a side step instead of turning around.

No Tension in the Handhold on Underarm Turns

You should have no tension in the handhold on underarm turns. Do not hang onto one another during the turn. Let the connection break if you cannot maintain contact comfortably. Do not put stress on the turning person's shoulder.

Keep Your Hand Where the Turning Person Can Reach

The non-turning person should put their hand over their partner's head where their partner can maintain contact. Do not attempt to keep the same connection throughout the turn. Allow the turning person's hand to turn freely.

Bring Your Hands Back to Proper Position After Turning

> At a West Coast swing workshop, we were practicing a sugar tuck turn. The instructor rotated to me. After the turn, the instructor did a double-take. She was surprised we ended in the same handhold we started. Everyone else ended with the man's hand awkwardly on top of the woman's.

When you finish the turn, the man should bring his hand directly back to his desired hand position. The woman simply puts her hand back in the man's hand. You should have a natural handhold when finished with your turn. If your handhold is awkward, you did something wrong.

Close the Distance for Underarm Turns

Whoever is turning is the vulnerable person. The other person should close the distance so that the turning person can comfortably maintain hand contact. When your partner turns under your arm, do whatever you have to do to stay close to your partner. Staying close to your partner is your priority for safety sake. If you must, chase after your partner during the turn, otherwise, let the connection break.

Reach Up on Underarm Turns

When your partner turns under your arm, do not reach out, reach up. No matter how short you are, as long as you are close to your partner, if you reach straight up, you can reach over almost every partner's head.

Prepare the Turn First

You should put yourselves in a position to turn before you turn. Both partners should be ready for the turn ahead of time.

Prepare With Contra Body Movement

You can use contra body movement to prepare for turns. In open position, if you step with contra body movement, you prepare yourself to turn first one way and then another. As you come forward, your hips already begin the rotation. The man can lead this contra body movement. If the man is not leading contra body movement, the woman can optionally walk with contra body movement to prepare herself.

Abort If Out of Position

If you are out of position, you can get hurt attempting to turn. Do not rush into a turn. If you cannot comfortably do a turn, abort.

The Man Only Initiates the Turn for the Woman

The man does not lead the woman through her turn. The man cannot control the speed at which the woman turns. Attempting to control the woman through an underarm turn would put stress on her shoulder as well as risk throwing her off balance. For safety sake, you should refrain from trying to control the woman's turn.

Lead the Turn With Horizontal Movement of the Connection

You lead the turn by moving the connection horizontally. For underarm turns, you can start the woman turning with the hand below the woman's head, at waist height, or elsewhere, by moving the connection sideways. Once the woman starts to rotate, you can then move the hand above her head. Alternatively, you can first raise the hand above her head. Then move the connection horizontally. Do not move the hand diagonally from down low to up high to lead the turn. If you are late, abort.

Get the Hand Up Early

To lead the underarm turn, get the hand up early. Do not wait for the step when the woman turns to raise her hand. Have the hand up early enough to allow the woman to prepare herself for the turn.

Lead the Turn With Your Body

> While reviewing a salsa demonstration video I had made, I noticed my partner started to turn her head almost two steps before I initiated the turn with my hand. I had subconsciously led the turn with my body, which was why she was able to do the turn so naturally.

The best way to lead turns is with your body, not your hands. Think about how you can first prepare, then initiate the woman's rotation by moving your body.

Turning for the Woman

There are two types of turns for women. One is turning in place. The other is turning after you started to step, which is a traveling turn. You can execute turns in any way that you like as long as you end where you are supposed to end. You can turn as fast or as slow as you want. You can turn as many times as you like.

Half Turn per Step

While you can turn in any way that you like, the man is typically asking you to turn halfway on each step. You should step on the same line when you turn halfway, whether you are turning in place or traveling. By turning halfway, you keep your hips aligned with your position, which stabilizes your turn. If you turn less than halfway, you will be in your own way on your next step. Your supporting hip will be blocking your free foot. You will need to take additional steps to get all the way around. If you turn more than halfway, you may have a tendency to spin out of control.

Turning in Place

When the leader invites you to turn in place, you should end where you started. You may end facing a different direction if the leader stops you in a new direction.

Traveling Turns

When you turn while traveling, you turn then step, or step then turn. Each step should be on the line on which you are traveling.

Turn Right on Right, Left on Left

The easiest way to turn is to turn right when standing on your right foot and to turn left when standing on your left foot. When you turn this way, you can see where you are going. You are turning in your forward-facing direction. Your free hip only has to travel about a quarter of the way around before you can step down your line after your turn.

Turn Left on Right, Cross in Front

> After a couple of years, in our swing dancing class, Jim asked me why the women could not do something. I told Jim, "Because they do not cross in front."
>
> Jim said, "But you taught them that the very first day."
>
> I replied, "And every day thereafter for the last two years."

When you turn left on your right foot or right on your left foot, you are turning backward. Turning backward is common but is more difficult. You cannot see where you are going. The back of your head is leading your turn. Your free hip has to travel about three-quarters of the way around before you can step down your line. In some dances, you cross your left foot in front of your right instead of turning backward. You are effectively turning left on left. You turn facing forward. You do not have to bring your free hip all the way around before you can step. Crossing in front is quicker. Crossing in front keeps you on your line.

Turn Your Head First

When you get the signal to turn, especially if you are only doing a half-turn, you can turn your head first. Turning your head lets you look in the direction of your turn. Turning your head helps to bring your body around first which helps you turn faster. Turning your head helps keep the connection relaxed.

Let the Parts of Your Body Move Separately

When doing a half-turn while traveling, try not to turn like a refrigerator with all the parts of your body locked in place. In an underarm turn, try not to lock your overhead arm to your opposite hip so that your arm does not move unless your hip moves. Your hips have a long way to go. Your hips turn slow. When you lock your arm to your hip, you tend to fight with your leader in the connection. You turn like a big block of wood. Try to let the parts of your body move separately. First turn your head, looking back at the direction where you will end facing. Relax your arm. Let your arm come down and around. Let the rest of your body unravel with your upper body turning first, followed by your hips.

Point Your Toes in the Direction of Your Turn

> Nose follows toes. ~ Maria Alvarez, ballroom dance instructor

Point your toes in the direction of your turn. There will be times when you turn your head first. There will be times when you turn your toes first. There will be times when you turn your hips first. There are many ways to turn. Be aware of the needs of your position.

Three-Step Spot Turn Basketball Pivot

In some social dances, you do a three-step spot turn using a basketball pivot. You take your first step away from your where you are standing. You make a basketball pivot. You finish where you started. You should take your first step on the line on which you are dancing. This usually will be either in line with your partner or perpendicular to your partner.

Three-Step Traveling Turn

In some social dances, you do a three-step traveling turn. Your three-step turn may result in a full turn or a turn one and a half times around. On one of the steps, you turn facing forward, turning right on right or left on left. That is your easy step. On another step you turn backward, turning right on left or left on right. That is your harder step. Stay on your line on all three steps, so that all three steps travel in the same direction down the line. Do not turn your traveling turn into a spot turn.

Keep Your Feet Close Together on Traveling Turns

When you turn while traveling, for better balance, keep your steps close together. The smaller your steps, the tighter your turn. You have more control over your turn. You turn faster.

Spotting

When turning, you can look at a spot while you turn. You can look straight ahead at a spot in the direction that you are going. Or, you can look at two spots, one ahead and one behind. Rather than moving your head as your body turns, you keep your head steady. As you do your turn, you whip your head around to keep looking at a spot. This may help you to stabilize your turn.

Dizziness

You may wonder how some people can keep turning without getting dizzy. The answer is training. Your brain learns from your behavior. The more you turn, your brain learns to handle the stimulus from turning. When your brain learns that you know what you are doing, your brain stops making you feel dizzy.

Pirouettes Are Not Expected

Turns must be easy enough for a normal person to be able to do. A pirouette, spinning all the way around on one foot, is too hard to expect someone to be able to do. If you have the skill, pirouette away.

Turning in Closed Position With Your Partner

Turning with your partner is more difficult than turning by yourself. You cannot use your partner to help you turn. When you turn with your partner, you need to be able to execute your part of the turn without hanging onto your partner for support.

Counterbalancing While Turning

While at times you may wish to counterbalance while turning, there is no counterbalancing in social dancing. Leaning back into your partner's hand for support is perilous. You should not take the decision to whirl your partner around on your own. If you want to counterbalance, ask permission from your partner first. Practice with your partner ahead of time. Make sure you can do so safely.

Turning Around the Center Between the Partners

When you turn with your partner, you can both go around a point between each other. In this case, the center point stays in place. Both partners move the same amount around the center.

Traveling Around Your Partner

Another way you can turn is for one partner to go around the other. One person stays in the center, changing their facing direction. The other person goes around the person in the center.

Traveling Through Your Partner

Yet another way is to go through your partner's position traveling down the floor. The person going forward, goes through their partner's position, turning around to face backward. The person facing backward gets out of the way, then steps back in facing forward. You reverse positions, having traveled while you turn.

He Goes She Goes Traveling Turn

When you travel while you turn, you alternate who goes around whom. You do half turns with each iteration as you travel down the floor. The partner behind goes past their partner in the front. As the partner in the front passes, the partner in the center puts their foot between the legs of their partner going by.

Disassociate To Let Your Partner Pass

You must disassociate to allow your partner to pass by you. The man leads by rotating his upper body to ask the woman to pass. The woman disassociates to maintain the connection as the man passes. For both, as your partner passes, you can then step between their legs.

Right When Right, Left When Left

When turning to the right, your right foot goes between your partner's feet. When turning to the left, your left foot goes between your partner's feet. When traveling counter-clockwise around the room, turning to the right is easier because the traveling person is moving a shorter distance along the inside of the circle. When turning left, the traveling person is moving a longer distance along the outside of the circle. At the end of your left turn, you may need to cross your left in front of your right to get back in front of your partner.

Alter the Timing

Often, you have to alter the timing of your footwork when you turn with your partner. If you both step on the beat at the same time, you may be in each other's way. The man often has to alter his timing to allow the woman to take her step first, allowing her to pass by before he can take his step. At times, the same applies to the woman. In either case, the man allows the woman to step on the beat.

Traveling Pivot Turns

A traveling pivot turn is when you make about a half turn on each step. You travel down the floor together, making a full turn in two steps. Doing two pivot turns in a row may be the most difficult step in social dancing. Perhaps pivot turns are too difficult to expect someone to be able to do in social dancing. In doing a pivot turn, when your partner is going past you, you need to rotate, while balancing over your standing leg, sitting back to keep your body out of the way of your partner. As your partner steps past you, you step forward through your partner's leg, past your partner's foot down the line of dance. You make less than a half turn when you step past your partner. You make more than a half turn when you rotate to step through your partner. This is easier to do counterbalancing because you can sit back, but counterbalancing is not social dancing. Rather than step through their partner, some men bring both their feet together when they rotate. You do what you can.

Points To Remember

1. Maintain your posture while turning.

2. Do not turn and step at the same time.

3. No tension in the handhold on underarm turns.

4. Close the distance for underarm turns.

5. Reach up on underarm turns.

6. Prepare the turn first.

7. Abort if out of position.

43. Turning

8. The man only initiates the turn for the woman.

9. Lead the turn with horizontal movement of the connection.

10. Get the hand up early.

11. Lead the turn with your body.

12. Half turn per step.

13. Turn right on right, left on left.

14. Turn left on right, cross in front.

15. Turn your head first.

16. Let the parts of your body move separately.

17. Point your toes in the direction of your turn.

18. Keep your feet close together on traveling turns.

19. Disassociate to let your partner pass.

20. Right foot forward when turning right, left when left.

21. Alter timing as needed when turning together.

44. Leader Skills

> Give me time to finish my pivot. ~ Joan Frosch,
> University of Florida dance professor

Here are some tips for the men to keep in mind.

You Are a Team

Let your partner do her own dancing. Do not try to control your partner. Resist the temptation to coerce your partner. Invite your partner. Cooperate with your partner to create inspirational moments.

Get Her in the Mood

When you first make a connection, allow her to synchronize with you. Relax. Take a deep breath. Allow her to settle in the connection.

Lead With Your Body

Think about leading with your body, not your hands. Use your body to move your hands, when that makes sense.

Straight for Straight, Around for Turn

When you want the woman to step, move the connection straight in the direction you want her to step. When you want the woman to turn, move the connection around the woman.

Be Subtle

You only need to move the connection a tiny amount to get the woman moving. When the woman has started moving, your job is done. Once in motion, the woman will do the rest.

Move With Authority

> When I was first learning to dance with a partner, I asked the teacher to lead me. I was stunned by how he got me to move where he wanted without doing anything to me. He created a space with his frame which compelled me to move into without pushing me.

Be clear about what you are inviting the woman to do. Specifically, you are asking her to go straight or turn. Be clear without being controlling. Move your body with authority. Move your body into the space you want to occupy so your partner knows where to move.

Wait Until the Woman Is Ready

Before doing anything, make sure you are in position to do the movement well. Wait until the woman is ready for you to lead her. Prepare the woman for the upcoming movement. If you are not properly prepared for whatever you are going to do, take extra time to get in the appropriate position.

Affecting the Woman's Balance

> A guy came to my class who had been dancing salsa. A woman was having trouble following him, so I asked him to lead me. He was impossible for me to follow. He was trying to turn me without regard to what I was doing. While I was stepping forward, he was trying to turn me in another direction.

Being able to intentionally affect the woman's balance is the essential skill in leading. You need to understand how the woman is balanced. You move so that the woman's response to your movement is what you want. Remember, you are not moving the woman. You are moving the parts on your body to which the woman is connected. The woman responds to your movement by stepping or rotating.

Allow the Woman To Move With You

> I was leading dancing as an evening activity for an outdoor club. One of the ladies was a salsa dancer. Within just a few moments after we started dancing, she said, "Wow, you are a really good dancer." We had not done anything more than the basic step. She was used to men yanking her around instead of dancing with her.

Move in a way that allows the woman to move with you. If the woman is starting from a standstill, get her moving slowly at first to initiate her movement. If the woman is already moving, first coordinate your movement to hers, catching her movement, and then redirecting to where you want her to go.

Time Your Signals With the Woman's Weight Changes

To make your leads part of the woman's natural movement, you must time your signals with the woman's weight changes.

Signal Early

Signal the woman early. Give the woman the time she needs to execute her movements comfortably.

Free the Appropriate Foot for the Woman

> I had the hardest time letting the woman know which foot to stand on.

Before you start dancing, let the woman know which foot to move. Position the connection so that the woman must stand on one leg, freeing the leg with which you want her to take her first step. Make sure you know which is the woman's free foot. If you are unsure, move the connection so that the woman switches her weight from foot to foot until you are sure.

Move Your Body Before Your Foot

> I was such a slow learner that my friend Gordon said to me, "What is taking you so long?" I could not get the woman to move out of the way without stepping on her.

Do not kick your partner with your foot before she has a chance to move. The woman is in contact with your body, not your foot. To signal her to move early, move your body first. She will naturally start to move in the direction indicated.

Move Your Body Across Your Foot

> My dance teacher wanted to give up on me many times. She complained, "I cannot teach you to dance. You have no core."

When you want to move forward, start with your weight over the sturdy part of your foot. Move your body weight forward over your foot. You only need to inch forward to signal the woman. She will clearly feel your body coming forward. She will move her leg out of the way so you have room to step.

Use Your Behind

> No matter how often I felt like giving up, I figured if I persisted, I would eventually learn.

Do not pitch yourself forward as if you are falling over. Move your body forward with your muscles. Flex your rear end to move your body forward, across your foot, so you stay supported during your initial movement. You only need to get your motion started. This tells your partner to move out of your way, freeing the space for you to move into.

Put the Woman's Weight Down

I just kept showing up each week. One day I was better.

When moving the connection horizontally, you can first raise the connection a slight amount. As you continue to move the connection horizontally, the woman continues to reach with her free leg. When her foot is where you want, you can lower the connection as you stop the horizontal movement. You can also first lower and then raise the connection as well. This slight lifting and lowering is useful for indicating the length of steps.

Points To Remember

1. You are a team.

2. Resist the temptation to coerce your partner.

3. Invite your partner.

4. Lead with your body.

5. Straight for straight, around for turn.

6. Be subtle.

7. Move with authority.

8. Wait until the woman is ready.

9. Move with the woman, allow the woman to move with you.

10. Time your signals with the woman's weight changes.

11. Signal early.

12. Free the appropriate foot for the woman.

44. Leader Skills

13. Move your body across your foot.

14. Use your behind.

45. Follower Skills

> Ray might sound like he is contradicting me, but we are
> both getting to the same point from different directions.
> ~ Maria Alvarez, ballroom dance instructor

Here are some tips for women to keep in mind.

Focus on Connection

Do not worry about what steps to do. Focus on the connection. Maintain your frame. Keep your posture. Try to balance over each step. Your steps will come of their own. In this way, you can follow even a bunch of fast steps.

Look Where You Are Going

You should look straight ahead most of the time. Turning your head turns your body. This is a problem when you turn your head to look at your partner when he has stepped to the side. Generally, you should look where you are going, not at your partner, unless you are facing your partner.

Dance Downhill

Follow your balance. Do not use your eyes. Do not guess. Do not dance figures. Move in the way that feels natural. Dance like you are dancing downhill.

Resistance Is Futile

Do not resist the movement of your partner. Your objective is to move with your partner as light as a feather. Any resistance, besides being uncomfortable and possibly dangerous, loses information creating ambiguity.

Start Standing on One Foot or the Other

You need to be on one foot or the other at the beginning of each step. If you are standing on two feet, you cannot move. You have to shift your weight to one foot to be able to step with the other. If you do not know which foot you should be standing on, pick one. Be clear about which foot you are standing on. Your partner needs to know which foot you have free. He can then adjust accordingly.

Do Not Change Weight on Your Own

You should stand on the foot the leader signaled you to stand on. If you do not know which foot, stay on the foot you are on. Do not change weight on your own.

Wait for Your Leader

The man goes first. The woman follows the man. Wait for your man to move. Coordinate your movement to his throughout the entire length of your step.

Do Not Fall Backward

You step backward a lot. When the man initiates your backward step, if you move your upper body back first, you will start to fall over backward. To keep from falling, you will cut your step short. You will block the man's forward step. You may get stepped on.

Do Not Fall Sideways

When the man initiates your sidestep, if you move your upper body sideways first, you will start to fall sideways. To keep from falling, you will take some random length sidestep. You will not be able to determine the length of the step the man wants you to take.

Wait To Put Your Free Foot Down

When the man starts to move, you should not step right away because you do not know how far to step. Keep your upper body in place. Keep your weight on your supporting leg. Wait to put your free foot down until the man indicates for you to do so.

Absorb the Man's Movement in Your Frame

When the man starts to move, you do not know how far he wants you to go. Relax your frame to absorb the man's movement so that you are not forced off-balance. Delay your upper body movement until you see where the man wants you to go. When you move, return your frame to your normal position.

Extend Your Leg

> When the leader starts to move the connection, extend your free leg. ~ Ilana, Argentine tango instructor

When the man initiates your movement, whether forward, back, or side, start to extend your leg in the direction indicated. Keep your weight on your standing leg. Continue to extend your leg until the man indicates the length of your step.

Point Your Toe

When your partner initiates stepping into you, you must move your leg out of the way so your partner has a place to step. Bending at the knee to move your foot back is not enough. Point your toe to move your thigh out of the way so your partner's knee does not hit you. Think about extending your leg from your hip, or even from your rib cage, to get your leg out of the way.

Push Off Your Front Foot

If your partner is stepping into you, make space on the floor to allow your partner to step into. Push off your front foot to extend your step. Wait for your partner to indicate to put your free foot down. If you put your foot down after the man, you cannot get stepped on, at least not on that foot.

Trust Your Balance

Do not do what you think the man wants you to do. Follow where your balance takes you. If this was not what your leader intended, you will give him the feedback he needs to understand how his movement affected you.

Stay in the Embrace, Do Not Curve the Room

In traveling dances, the couple moves around the floor. When approaching a corner, the couple typically rounds out the corner, traveling in an oval shape. Women tend to lead around the corners, curving the room, forcing the men to follow them. You should not lead the man around the corners. Stay in the man's frame. You can check yourself in this circumstance by keeping your nose to your left of your partner's nose.

Points To Remember

1. Focus on connection.

2. Look where you are going, not at your partner.

3. Dance downhill.

4. Start standing on one foot or the other.

5. Do not change weight on your own.

6. Wait for your leader.

7. Extend your leg.

8. Absorb the man's movement in your frame.

9. Do not let your partner bump knees with you.

10. Point your toe.

11. Push off your front foot.

12. Trust your balance.

13. Stay in the embrace, do not curve the room.

46. Develop Your Skill

> To get better, you have to keep practicing the simple, foundational basics. You have to do them enough so they come out automatically when you dance. ~ Daniela Pucci, Argentine tango professional instructor

A lot of getting better is simply about time. Your body has to learn the nuances of moving with a partner. As long as you are not developing bad habits, you get better by dancing. The more you dance, the better you get.

Reaching Limits

> I have a friend who is an excellent, social, Argentine tango dancer. The ladies love to dance with him. He can do all the things he needs to do. He is unaware that he does not transfer his weight when he steps. Until he learns this skill, he will be unable to take his dancing to the next level.

If you are only dancing, without going to class, you may not learn new skills. You may reach limits that you cannot pass because you do not have the necessary, foundational skills. To continue to grow your dancing, you have to acquire new skills.

Find the Right Exercises

> During class, I was practicing bachata with a woman. She was fine going side to side. When going forward and back, she had trouble, taking an extra step. I told her to focus on the connection, to relax her arms, soften her handhold, and to let her steps come naturally. She was unable to do any of those things. She kept trying to watch me. She kept doing her steps on her own. I told

her to close her eyes. After a short time, a transformation took place. Since she no longer had her eyes to depend on, she naturally had to do all the things I asked her to do. Her hands relaxed, she balanced over each step, and she waited for me. She moved with me, doing her steps with mine.

You have to find the right exercises. Good instruction allows you to improve faster by providing you with exercises that force you to use sound fundamentals.

Practice Your Basics

I have been doing this dance for 30 years. Every day, I still practice my basic half turn. ~ Katie Marlow, Hustle world champion

You get better by practicing. Practicing good exercises trains your body to move properly when you dance. Keep improving your basics. Everything else will follow.

Putting What You Learned To Work for You

I was at a Latin club in South Florida. Since I rarely dance salsa, rather than doing fancy moves, I kept things simple. I just tried to connect with my partner and the music without pushing and pulling.

The woman I was dancing with said to me, "You are a really good salsa dancer."

I shrugged off her compliment.

She was intent on making her point. She stopped dancing, looked at me, and said, "No really. I am not just saying that. I dance salsa a lot, with all the best dancers, and you are a really good salsa dancer."

South Florida is the heart of salsa dancing so she must know what she is talking about. I do not think of myself as a good salsa dancer. I have no Latin style. I was simply following the ABCDs in this book.

Put the tools you have learned to work for you. Go have a good time.

Points To Remember

1. The more you dance, the better you get.

2. Keep going to class to learn new skills.

3. Practice your basics.

4. Put the ABCDs to work for you. Go have a good time.

How To Dance With a Partner

* * *

Part Summary

47. Summary

> A step is either leadable or not, and if not, the step is not
> social dancing. ~ Jeff Subeck, Israeli and social dancer

In this chapter, you review the method of communicating every step in every dance.

The Method of Communicating Every Step

Use the mnemonic ABCD to help you remember the important points.

A. Attitude

B. Balance

C. Connection

D. Direction

A for Attitude

> Sometimes I feel like staying home but I force myself to
> go dancing anyway. I have never been sorry I did so.
> Once I get to dancing, I am always glad I went. ~ Richard,
> social dancer

Your attitude plays the most important role in your enjoying your experience.

1. Follow the social values of safety, courtesy, and comfort.

   Safety - Do not hurt yourself or anyone else. Everyone does their own dancing. Everyone moves their own body parts.

   Courtesy - Be considerate. Do not tell anyone else what to do.

Comfort - Be physically and emotionally comfortable. You are responsible for your own comfort. Tell your partner what you need.

2. Follow the dance values of teamwork, natural, and freedom.

   Teamwork - Dancing is a team sport. The man invites and the woman completes. The man's responsibilities are: position the couple on the dance floor, keep time with the music, and initiate the choreography. The woman's responsibilities are: keep time with the man, maintain the connection, and complete her choreography.

   Natural - Be natural. If anything is unnatural, rethink what you are doing.

   Freedom - Maximize freedom of movement. Maximize freedom of expression.

   Remember men, invite the woman to move. Avoid coercing her. Lead what you want. Be happy with what you get.

   Remember ladies, follow, follow, follow. The answer to most any question the man asks is, "I do not know. You are leading." Your job is not to keep the ship from sinking. Your job is to go down with the ship.

3. Keep in mind the communication requirements: clearly defined, easy, fast, and universal. Your communication must be logical, precise, and unambiguous. Social dancing must be simple enough for a normal person to learn to do. Your communication must be fast enough to do in time to the music. You communicate in the same way with every person in every social dance.

47. Summary

If anything you are doing violates any of the ten values, something is wrong. Look deeper into what you are doing. Try some other way to accomplish what you want.

B for Balance

The Law of Balance: everyone maintains their own balance.

1. Balance is the most important skill in dancing.

2. No pushing and no pulling, not even a little.

3. The woman must maintain her posture to define her position.

4. The two horizontal movements are step and rotate.

C for Connection

The Law of Connection: the woman maintains the connection.

The Rule of Frame: the woman maintains her frame when the man moves the connection horizontally, otherwise she lets her frame adjust.

Rule of Plane of Communication: horizontal communication is for horizontal movement. Vertical communication is for vertical movement.

1. The woman's position is defined by the connection and the woman's frame.

2. Raising the hand does not mean turn. Vertical movement adjusts the frame, if possible.

3. Stillness means stay still. Motion means to move.

4. Free position is when you are not touching your partner. The woman follows visually when not physically connected.

5. Open position is when you are not in an embrace. The woman follows all the points of the connection.

6. Closed position is when you are in an embrace. The woman connects with the man's body. The woman follows the connection she made with the man's body. In open embrace, the woman places her left hand on the front of the man's right shoulder. In close embrace, the woman connects with her sternum on the man's body.

D for Direction

The Law of Direction: the woman maintains her direction.

1. The three directions for the woman are straight, turn, and circle.

2. The basic patterns that make up all figures are go straight, turn in place, walk around in a circle, and turn while traveling.

3. The woman stops when her movement is blocked or she reaches the end of her connection.

4. The man only initiates the woman's movement.

5. The woman completes her movement on her own.

6. The man waits for the woman to complete her movement.

7. When going straight or circling, the woman takes every step on her line of dance.

8. For turn while traveling, the woman goes straight, turns, then finishes going straight.

9. During a traveling turn, the woman makes a half-turn with each step.

10. Whoever is going backward is responsible for getting out of the way so they do not get their free foot stepped on.

Technique

To lead and follow every step, you need to be balanced. You need to transfer your weight so you can coordinate your step.

Use These Ideas as Powerful Tools

There is knowledge and there is skill. You need the knowledge to acquire the appropriate skills. You acquire the skills by practice. Use these ideas to help you practice in a way that you steadily improve. Avoid developing bad habits.

You Have To Train Your Body

> You are training me to dance in the same way I train to ride horses. ~ Frida, beginning Argentine tango dancer and dressage competitor

You have to train your body to move the way you want. To be able to perform consistently in time to music takes practice. Focus on one skill at a time. Go as slow as necessary for you to perform the skill with proper form. Perform the skill repetitively to train your muscle memory. At some point, you will be able to do the skill automatically.

Points To Remember

1. Use the mnemonic ABCD.

2. A for Attitude. The ten values are safety, courtesy, comfort, teamwork, natural, freedom, clearly defined, easy, fast, and universal.

3. B for Balance. The Law of Balance: everyone maintains their own balance.

4. C for Connection. The Law of Connection: the woman maintains the connection. The Rule of Frame: the woman maintains her frame when the man moves the connection horizontally.

5. D for Direction. The Law of Direction: the woman continues her direction. The three directions are straight, turn, and circle. The woman stops when she reaches the end of her connection or her motion is blocked.

6. Transfer your weight.

48. Next Steps

> You paid your money, now dance. ~ Nissim Ben Ami, Israeli Folk dance instructor

Congratulations on getting to this point. Put your knowledge to good use. Go dancing.

Reread this book often. Read sections that interest you at the time. As your dancing progresses, you will have new insights.

Visit www.PartnerDancing.com

Go to the website now. On the website you can:

1. Pay for this book.

2. Sign up for the partner dancing newsletter.

3. Print the rules.

4. Get additional instruction.

Invite Others

Invite others to learn the ABCDs℠ of how to dance with a partner so you have more people to dance with.

How To Dance With a Partner

* * *

Appendix

Appendix Topics

> When you get your black belt, then you can start
> learning. ~ My martial arts instructor

The topics in this appendix are listed in alphabetical order with no regard for what order you should read them. Read them in whatever order they interest you. These topics are not essential to your learning how to dance with a partner. They provide supporting information for what you have already learned. They address areas of interest in social dancing. Some of the topics deserve far longer discussions. Here, the author shares some thoughts on these topics to bring them to the attention of readers.

Author Andrew Weitzen

Andrew Weitzen has been enamored with social dancing since he first saw Scott Annan's jaw-dropping robot during the first week of their freshman year at the University of Florida.

Andrew is an enthusiastic dancer, teacher, and organizer of recreational dancing. He dances everything from Argentine tango to zydeco for fun. He loves teaching beginners. He has taught over 5,000 dance classes. As he says, "You have to sow seeds to grow your community."

Andrew specializes in getting non-dancers dancing. He has been invited to community programs, folk festivals, club events, social activities, family programs, special-care facilities, religious observances, universities, high schools, and elementary schools.

Andrew has been a faithful promoter of dancing in North Florida, publishing two newsletters a week since 2005, one for folk and one for partner dancing. He ran the Gainesville Dance Association, an eclectic hot spot of social dancing with two to three programs daily of a score of different types of social dancing.

Andrew is a software developer. He has a Bachelor of Science Degree in Mathematics from the University of Florida. His college fraternity entered him and his fraternity's sweetheart in the university's dance marathon. So he was known as the dance man even back then. He was the high school chess champion in Alachua County. A competitive athlete, he has played in, captained, coached, refereed, taught, ran leagues, and organized sporting programs since he can remember. He played basketball for Gainesville High School.

He played in the first Jose Cuervo professional beach volleyball tournament in Florida. He ran the IBM Club sports programs for 3,000 families. He has applied these experiences to dancing.

The Gainesville Dance Association

From a note to the landlord Richard and Phoebe Miles:

Thank you for renting us the space.

You gave us a great price, which allowed us to start small and grow. Your support helped us provide a unique service, which I would like to tell you about, so you know how your contributions have benefitted the community. We have programs attended by people of all ages, from young children to seniors in their 80s+.

People come to Gainesville from all over North Florida to dance. We frequently hear people say they wish they had something similar in their cities. In the last month, we have had visitors from Tallahassee, Valdosta, Jacksonville, St. Augustine, Daytona, Ocala, Orlando, and Tampa. We also have guests from other parts of the country who take the opportunity to dance with us while visiting Gainesville.

I do not know of anywhere else that provides a more eclectic choice of dancing.

Here is a peek at our regular schedule:

1. Sundays: Monthly vintage waltz brunch, Sacred Groove meditative dance, swing, hustle

2. Mondays: Irish dance youth performance group, English country, Israeli

3. Tuesdays: Argentine tango, ballroom

4. Wednesdays: West Coast swing

5. Thursdays: Senior line dancing, salsa, social dance

6. Fridays: Ballroom, UF Argentine tango club, salsa and Latin dance socials

7. Saturdays: international Folk, monthly swing socials, twice monthly Argentine tango milongas

We also provide space to the Brazilian Cultural Arts Exchange who holds classes primarily for children, teens, and young adults. They teach Brazilian capoeira Luanda and samba on Tuesdays, Wednesdays, Thursdays, and Saturdays. They host a yearly Batizado festival, with visitors from Brazil, and all over the South.

We have hosted benefits including two Tango for the Cure weekends to raise awareness and funds for breast cancer research, one last month on September 29.

At the end of this month, we are running our second annual event to benefit C.A.R.D the University of Florida Center for Autism and Related Disabilities with world-class West Coast swing professional Jen DeLuca on October 27.

Last March, we ran a Gainesville Dance Festival with 18 dance teachers and 14 sessions, over 3 days.

When Maria Alvarez's Imperial Dance Studio closed after 30 years due to increased rents, we were able to provide a place for her ballroom teachers and students.

We have provided space to various young people running groups to help build leadership.

We teach classes every quarter for Santa Fe College Community Education. Our next series for them starts in November.

We have brought in world-class professionals from Argentina, Brazil, Great Britain, and around the United States. Our local instructors are wonderful as well, some with championship resumes.

People are astonished by the fantastic dance community we have created with thanks to you.

If you are in town, stop by, and check us out. I have attached our September and October schedules so you can see what has been going on at 308 West.

Once again, thank you so much.

Sincerely,
Andrew Weitzen

Choreographed Group Dances

> The swing dancers look down on line dancing because it
> is not partner dancing, but you can learn a lot from line
> dancing. ~ Mark Traynor, founder of Floor Play,
> awarded River City Swing's first Trailblazer award

In contra, country-western, English country, international folk,
Israeli, square, and many other types of dancing, you do
choreographed, group dances in lines, circles, and other formations.
There are informal group dances, vaguely known by the dancers, but
gamely attempted at parties, like the conga line and the hora. In these
dances, when you hold hands the possibility of danger lurks.

Keep the Ten Values

The rules for dancing with a partner work for group dances too,
making them safer and easier. The rules work because much of the
interaction between dancers is the same whether you are interacting
with one or many. The ten values of social dancing apply to
recreational dancing, as do the laws of balance, connection, and
direction.

You Are Not a Human Chain

When you dance with a group, you are not a human chain. Do not
hang onto others in an attempt to keep the line together. No one is
drifting out to sea. Let others go if they cannot keep up.

Do Not Try to Control Others

It is not your job to keep the line organized. Do not try to control the
people around you by slowing the person in front of you down so the
person behind you can keep up. If you are doing that, you are the
problem, not them.

Do Not Try To Help Others

> While visiting Chicago, one evening I went to an
> international folk dance. There was a big line of dancers.
> Even though I did not know the dance, I jumped in.
> Rather than attempting to get the steps right, I listened
> to the music. I did whatever steps came to me. I just tried
> to match the movement of those alongside me. One of
> the ladies next to me told me I needed to hang on tightly.
> She started to call out the steps. I was doing fine until
> she began bothering me, pulling me off balance and
> distracting me from the music.

When you try to help others you confuse them. Dancing is hard
enough without someone bothering you. Let others figure out what
to do for themselves.

Calling Steps Is Bad

Calling individual steps is bad. Too much information. You are not
playing Simon Says. You are distracting them from what they need to
focus on.

The Best Way To Help Others Is To Do What You Are Supposed To Do

The best way to help someone is for you to dance well so they can
copy what you are doing.

The Problem Is Skill, Not Knowledge

If you are a beginner, the problem is not that you do not know the
steps of a dance. You may learn the steps. You may even be able to
teach the steps. But, when the music comes on, you may still not be

able to do the steps. This is because dancing is not knowledge. Dancing is a physical skill.

You use a different part of your nervous system to dance than you do to think. Dancing happens too fast for thinking. When the music comes on, you do not have time to think about what to do. You use the part of your nervous system that responds automatically. You use your muscle memory. You do what you have been trained to do, or at least, what you have always done. If you do not have the necessary skills, even if you know the steps, you will not be able to do them in time to the music. You will be off-balance. You will be on the wrong foot. You will not be on the beat of the music.

Do Not Worry About Steps

Children can do every dance. The reason is they do not try to do the steps. They follow where you are going, not how you are stepping. They go forward, backward, left, right, and turn around, all without a problem. Similarly, novices can contra, English country, and square dance their first day because they follow directions, not steps, such as circle left and circle right. You can line, Israeli, and international folk dance your first day if you follow directions instead of steps.

Do Not Try To Get Everything, Try To Get Anything

You can still dance, even if you do not know how. You will learn. Do not try to get everything. Just try to get anything. Your group does the same dances every week. Try to get any part of the dance. Each week you will get a little more. Eventually, you will get the whole thing. Be patient. Enjoy the challenge.

Watching the Feet Is Bad

Do not follow by looking at feet. This causes you to have poor posture, throws you off balance, and disorients you.

The Feet Are for Moving the Body

Do not worry about steps. The feet are for moving the body. Move your body where you are supposed to go. Your feet will follow. If you are on the wrong foot, you are only off by one. Dance to the music. Eventually, your feet will fix themselves.

Focus on Fundamental Skills

Focus on fundamental dance skills. Pay attention to how you move. Maintain good posture. Do not look down. Look in the direction you are going. Understand your balance. Do not stand on two feet. Stand on one foot or the other. Change weight fully. Travel on a line. Keep your feet on the floor. Bring your knees and ankles together as you walk. Use contra body movement. Pivot over your supporting leg. Do not travel while you pivot. That makes you a wobbly top.

Learn To Dance by Learning Rhythms

Listen to the music. Learn the rhythms used in the dances you do. Train your body to move to each of the rhythms.

Learn the Elements

Learn the basic elements of the dances you do. The elements are sequences of steps done to a particular rhythm, such as a grapevine step. Practice the elements so you can do them automatically.

Leader and Followers

In group dancing, the leader is the head of a group. Everyone else are the followers. The leader is determined by the style of the dance. In a line of dancers, the leader is at the head of the line. In a closed circle, the leader is usually the teacher of the group. In group partner dancing, like contra, English, and square dancing, the man is the leader for the woman. The number one couple is the leader for the other couples. Everyone follows the leader.

The Law of Balance

The law of balance applies to groups. Everyone does their own dancing. Do not apply force to anyone else. Do not hang onto them. No reaching, no grabbing, no fiddling. Let everyone control their own body parts. Do not throw others off-balance. No pushing and pulling.

Keep Good Balance and Posture

You follow easier if you have good balance and posture. Move as described under balance. Move from your center. Allow the people next to you to feel your movement.

The Law of Connection

The law of connection works with groups. To follow, maintain the connection.

Orient Yourself and the Feet Will Follow

Follow by orienting yourself to the position. The easiest way to follow is to follow someone's body, not their feet. Orient yourself to the dancer in front of you. Go in the direction they are going. Stay on their shoulder. Align your shoulders to theirs. Your feet will naturally do the right thing if you go in the right direction.

Everyone Owns the Space They Are In

Do not run over anyone. If someone does not know the dance and is in your way, dance in place until that dancer moves on.

Do Your Job, Keep Up With the Person in Front of You

Your leader is the person in front of you. In a line or circle, you follow the person ahead of you. Keep up with that person. The person behind you follows you. You do not wait for the person behind you. It is their job to keep up with you.

Go Faster To Keep Up With Your Leader

The leader of your line sets the pace for the line. Maintain the connection with the dancer in front of you. If you cannot keep up, let go. If you feel tension in the connection with the dancer leading you that means you are going too slow. Move your feet. Go faster. If you feel tension in the connection with the dancer behind you, that dancer is not going fast enough. Let them go.

Handholds

Hold hands comfortably, like walking down the street, without tension. Be fully present in the handhold, without using thumbs to grip. In group dances, what handhold to make is not always obvious. Each time two dancers connect, they have to negotiate a handhold. Dancers tend to grope hands. This takes away from the beauty of everyone dancing together. Following are some handhold guidelines to cover most situations, so everyone knows what handhold to make. The leader presents the connection. The follower connects.

Use a Right Handshake Hold for Circle Dances

Use a right handshake hold for Balkan, Greek, Israeli, international, and other dancing that frequently travels in a circle counter-clockwise. To make the right handshake hold, extend your right hand, forward on the line, like you were shaking hands. Place your hand in your leader's left hand. Extend your left hand behind you, presenting the connection to your follower. For shoulder holds, use the right handshake in a similar way, by placing your right hand on your leader's left arm or shoulder.

Men Palms Up for Couples Dances in Lines and Squares

For couples dances in lines and squares, like contra, English, and square dancing, the existing protocol is the man places his hands with palms up. The woman places her hands palms down in the man's hands. The woman should wait for the man to present the connection first. I acquiesce here to the current convention, even though the right handshake hold is simpler. The right handshake hold avoids the need for the following Right Hand Rule.

Right Hand Rule

> Right Hand Rule: the right hand does what the right hand always does.

At times, two men or two women will hold hands and the question is what handhold do they make? My solution is to use the right hand rule. You do whatever you normally would do with your right hand and you adjust your left hand as needed. Therefore, in a contra dance when men join hands, their right palms are up. When women join hands, their right palms are down.

Hands Across

Another handhold made in contra, English, and square dancing, is joining hands across with one pair holding hands above the other pair. The leader, which is the number one man, goes first. The connection he makes should be on top. The second couple should join hands below.

Points To Remember

1. Let everyone does their own dancing.

2. Keep up with your leader.

3. Use the appropriate handhold.

Choreographed Partner Dances

Cyd, an experienced folk dancer, moved to town and joined our group. She was reluctant to follow when dancing the woman's part since she had always memorized dances. One day I put on the partner dance Rina, which while an Israeli dance, was inspired by a Mexican hat dance, and was unlike any other dances that we do. Erin, who had been dancing with me for years, followed Rina perfectly, with all the crazy moves, the very first time, with no instruction. Cyd said, "Now, I am a believer."

I invented the rules for dancing with a partner for Israeli partner dancing. The rules work for other choreographed partner dances, such as contra, English country, folk, international, mixers, Nordic, round, salsa rueda, square, and others. The problem with choreographed partner dances is people rely on both the men and women memorizing their parts. The people do not learn how to dance together. When you learn how to dance with a partner, you can communicate in choreographed partner dances. This lets you do every dance, whether or not you know the steps.

A Three-Legged Race

If you have ever participated in a three-legged race at a picnic, you know that if you and your partner fight for control, you fall on your face. To coordinate in a three-legged race, one of you leads and one follows.

A Test of Wills

In Israeli partner dancing, the man learns his part. The woman learns her part. Then the couple wrestles with one another to see who is right. That is a joke, but unfortunately not far from the case. Certainly, not everyone who dances choreographed dances exhibit these faults. However, I have seen wonderful dancers in other social dance settings, commit grievances in choreographed settings they would never do elsewhere.

In many groups, there are no rules for how you dance with your partner. There is no leading and following. The goal of having two partners dance as one is lost, replaced by the objective of getting the steps right. Each partner does what they think is best. Dances turn into tests of will. Couples wrestle with one another for control, like an uncoordinated three-legged race. At best, this is unpleasant. Worse, you could fall on your face.

Booking Ahead With Regular Partners

The problems are so severe that dancers are often only comfortable with their regular partners, who they arrange to dance with ahead of time. In a more sociable dance setting, dancers change partners every dance, so everyone gets to dance about the same amount. With booking ahead, those without regular partners have trouble getting dances. They can be left out of the partner dancing for an entire evening.

Couples Sitting Down When They Do Not Know the Dance

At an Israeli folk dance camp, a young couple was ahead of me. They were two of the best dancers. They usually danced in the center for everyone to follow. A dance came on that one of them did not know. They left the dance floor. There is something wrong when the best couples have to sit out.

Since couples do not know how to dance with one another, but have only memorized their parts, if one of the partners does not know the dance, even the best dancers do not know what to do. They sit out dances when either of them does do not know the choreography. When they are dancing with their regular group, this may not happen much, because they are familiar with the dances that are played. When they visit another group, they may not know many of the dances. They may have to sit out a lot. This is a shame.

The Woman Causes the Struggle

The woman causes the problem when she does not follow. At best, she does her own dancing, ignoring her partner, so you are dancing in close proximity, but not dancing as one. More frequently, she creates conflict, physically wrestling with her partner in an attempt to impose her will.

Manhandling

The man causes unpleasantness by attempting to physically control his partner. At best, attempting to physically control the woman, prevents her from effectively following. Worse, the man may be dangerous, manhandling the woman, throwing her off-balance, while forcing her through movements.

Confusing Your Partner

Both dancers can confuse their partner in misguided attempts to help, such as reaching for their partner, nudging their partner, or telling their partner what steps to do.

The Solution Is To Follow the Rules for Dancing With a Partner

I was at Machol Miami, a popular Israeli Dance camp in Ft. Lauderdale. I was dancing with Veronica, one of the women from my group. Veronica had only been dancing a couple of years. I had trained her, kicking and screaming, on how to dance with a partner. She had protested my insistence on following, asking "What I am supposed to do if you lead the wrong steps? Follow you or do the steps of the dance?"

At the dance camp, they played eight partner dances in the set we were doing, none of which she had ever heard before. I had been dancing with different women for every set. I danced with many women, some that teach their own groups, and some others that are considered among the better dancers, ones I am friends with, and have enjoyed dancing with for years. Nevertheless, Veronica did those eight partner dances, the very first time, without instruction, better than the other women did the dances they knew because Veronica was following. We danced together. We tried to dance as one, even when we did the wrong steps.

Once you learn how to dance with a partner, you can have fun doing every dance even when you do not know the steps. There is no contest between dancing with someone who is following your every movement versus dancing with someone who is walking through a memorized pattern. A woman who is walking through a memorized pattern can never match her movements precisely to her partner. While the woman who is following follows by matching her movements precisely to her partner.

Choreography Is for the Man

In our group, for the most part, we only teach the choreography to the men. The women are to follow. If a woman wants to know the choreography, we do show her. The choreography is not a secret, but we expect her to follow regardless of the choreography. The men learn to lead. The women learn to follow. The emphasis is on communication skills so the two people are dancing together as one. Since this cooperation is going on, new male dancers can do the dances without feeling pressured. They learn the dances faster. The women learn to do every partner dance without instruction. Even beginners can do every partner dance. As they acquire more skill, they can do the dances better.

Do Not Correct the Leader

> I was dancing with Rachil who was an excellent follower. She also was fun to dance with. Even though she knew the dances, she waited for me. She matched her movements to mine so we were dancing as one. You could not ask for a better dancer as a partner.
>
> There were spots in each dance that she sensed I was going to do the wrong thing. With the tiniest of signals, at exactly the right time, she conveyed to me the correct movement. The way she signaled me could not have been better. If a woman is to help a man in a choreographed dance, this would be the way to do so. Since that day, I have been wondering, should a woman do that? The answer has to be no.

The woman helps herself by thinking the man is always doing the correct choreography. She can relax. She can enjoy the experience without worrying if her partner is doing the right steps. Your job as a follower is to follow, not to judge. Regardless of how gently you might do so, the woman does not signal the man to communicate choreography.

The Woman has Options

> At one point in the dance, I was supposed to turn Rachil one way. At just the right moment, to my surprise, she turned the other way in a more advanced maneuver.

The woman is free to dance however she likes. The man does not control the woman. The man only invites the woman to move. If she wants to do something else, she is free to do so.

Changing Partners

In our group, we like to change partners. We rotate, so everyone gets to dance with everyone else. Everyone gets to dance the same amount. Feels sociable. Seems fair. However, changing partner is not required.

No Gender Bias

Our group is not gender biased. Anyone can dance either role. Whoever is dancing the man's role leads. Whoever is dancing the woman's role follows.

Do the Dance More Than Once

If we do have dancers that sit out a dance because they do not have a partner, we may repeat the dance, changing partners first, so everyone gets to do the dance.

What To Do When the Man Does Not Know the Dance

As long as someone in the room knows the dance, the man follows those that know the dance. His partner follows him. Do what is easy. Skip steps to keep up. Avoid being out of control. Each time through the dance, you will pick up something else. The laws of dancing with a partner still apply. The man must be careful to only signal the woman. He must not force her through her movements. Resist the temptation to physically coerce your partner.

The woman must focus on her man. She must respond to his lead. She must be where he expects. The man will not be paying much attention to her, since he is trying to figure out what to do. She must avoid looking at what another couple is doing. If she pays attention to anyone other than her partner, he will notice that she is not responding to him. The man will get overloaded from the difficulty of trying to locate his partner while trying to follow another couple. This is too much for the man. This stresses the man. He will give up on that particular dance. He will sit down. To keep the man dancing, when he does not know the dance, the woman simply has to pay attention to him and only him. Women, if you want your man to keep dancing, follow him.

What To Do When the Woman Knows the Dance and the Man Does Not

When the woman knows the dance and the man does not, she should still follow the man. The woman cannot lead the man's steps. Since they will not be able to do the dance anyway, they might as well dance together. This way the man will eventually learn to do the dance. This is a small investment. After a few times through a dance, the man will know some of the steps. After a few sessions, the man will know much of the dance. If the woman tries to lead, the man will never learn the dance.

Points To Remember

1. Dance choreographed partner dances like you would any partner dance, follow the laws of dancing with a partner.

2. Be fair to everyone. Make your group more sociable. Rotate partners. Do dances more than once.

3. When the man does not know a dance, he follows a couple that knows the dance. The woman follows him.

4. The woman follows the man even when she knows the steps and he does not.

Choreography

Choreography is an essential learning tool in social dancing.

Master the Basic Elements

To dance reasonably close to the way others expect, learn the basic elements. The most basic elements of choreography are typically two to three steps long, with the timing of a measure of music or less. You should master the basic elements with the least excess movement. Mastering the basic elements builds a foundation on which to improve.

Fundamental Figures Are for Training

The basic elements comprise the fundamental figures of a dance. The fundamental figures form the structure of a dance. The fundamental figures are the length of one to two measures of music, two measures being a musical phrase. The figures have specific steps to specific rhythms. Dance teachers teach these figures. You should learn the fundamental figures of a dance. You should learn to execute the figures as instructed. Executing the figures with precision trains you in the skills needed for that dance.

Figures Are Optional

The figures have no special authority. You have the option of interpreting the music however you like. You are not restricted to a particular set of figures.

Routines Are Useful for Practice When You Vary the Choreography

Dance teachers often string together figures to make routines. Routines are useful for practice, provided you mix up the choreography. If you do the routine as shown, you do not know if you led and followed the steps. You may have been able to do the steps only because you knew them ahead of time. The man should alter the routine to ensure you are leading and following. The woman should follow her man. She should not do the routine automatically. The woman should also alter the choreography when she has the option to do so. This way you will know whether you are communicating the movements properly.

Do Not Dance Figures, Dance What Is Led

You do not dance figures. You lead and follow the signals for go straight, turn, and circle. You dance what is communicated by your partner. Both leaders and followers have options. Be aware of what options your partner is choosing. Respond appropriately. By following the method in this book, you will understand what you should be doing with your partner.

Add Variations To Improvise to Music

The fundamental figures for a dance, provide the foundation for variations. Most dances have only a handful of foundational figures. You can learn these figures in a short time. Once you can do your foundational figures, you can add variations to improvise to the music. You add variations in many ways, such as adjusting handholds, altering the movement, changing starting and ending positions, shorting or lengthening steps, adding styling, and applying syncopations.

Points To Remember

1. Master the basic elements.

2. Learn the fundamental figures with precision.

3. Figures have no special authority.

4. Vary practice routines so you know you are leading and following.

5. Do not dance figures. Dance what is led.

6. Variations let you improvise to the music.

Circle Direction

> My dance teacher was showing us how to lead the woman around in a circle by pulling her with one hand while nudging her on her back with the other.

Since the only things you can do when standing on one leg is step and rotate, all figures must be made of these two movements. Yet, the method in this book has three directions. The first two directions of straight and turn correspond to step and rotate, so no problem there. The issue is with the third direction circle. How does circle fit in?

To make a circle, you must rotate after each step. If there was no circle pattern, the man would lead a circle by leading each step followed by a small rotation. This does work. This is what people typically do who do not know the method in this book. However, leading a circle by leading each step is cumbersome. The method in this book adds the circle as a direction to simplify dancing with a partner.

The circle direction is somewhat arbitrary. You could make up other directions. However, in social dancing today, the only direction used besides straight and turn is the circle. Walking in a circle around your partner, called circling, and walking away from and back to your partner, called a walk-around turn, are common in many dances. While not as common as straight and turn, circle is common enough that adding circle as a direction is beneficial.

The circle direction raises interesting possibilities for new choreography, that of dancing on a circle instead of a line. Once on the circle, signals forward and back could indicate movement on the circle, instead of indicating a new straight line. The man could then send the woman back along the circle. She would travel along the circle in the opposite direction from the man, where he could meet her on the other side of the circle. There would be a need to make a rule for when to end the circle and return forward and back to a straight line.

Appendix

As of now, once the woman completes her movement on the circle her circle is done. She starts fresh with the next movement. Forward and back indicate a new straight line, not a circle.

If dancing on a circle is a possibility, dancing on other shapes could be as well, such as a square or diamond. You could arrange to do this with your partner beforehand.

Closed Position Open Embrace

Lead with your body not your hand.

The Woman's Left Hand Is on the Front of the Man's Right Shoulder

In closed position, the partners form an embrace. Closed position is characterized by the woman making connection with the man's body. The man leads the woman with this body connection. The standard position in closed position open embrace is with the man's right hand on the woman's left shoulder blade. The woman's left hand is on the front of the man's right shoulder. Other positions are possible but problematic. Some issues are discussed here.

Leading With the Woman's Left Hand in Another Position

When the woman's left hand is not on the front of the man's right shoulder, the man should still lead the woman as he always does, as if her hand was in the standard position. The man should not attempt to alter his lead to accommodate the woman's non-standard position. An exception being when the woman needs to alter the position of the connection due to injury or comfort, the man should do what is necessary to accommodate her.

Following With the Woman's Left Hand in Another Position

In closed position, the woman's rule is to follow the connection she made with the man's body. This presumes her hand is on the front of the man's shoulder in the standard position. If she places her hand somewhere else, she must dance as if she had her hand on the front of the man's left shoulder. If her hand is in a non-standard position, she will feel something different than what the man intends her to do. She must have the experience to know what to do, rather than following what she feels.

Breaking Connection With the Woman's Hand in Another Position

The man has two ways to break the open embrace. One is to release the embrace by removing his right hand from the woman's shoulder blade. The second, more common means, is to send the woman out of the embrace. When sending the woman out with the woman's hand on the front of the man's shoulder, the woman's hand naturally releases the connection. In other positions, the natural release may not happen. The woman needs to know to release her hand. For example, if the woman's hand is behind the man's shoulder, she will tend to pull on the man's back, causing her to turn to her left to face the man, instead of her going out from the embrace. If she has enough experience, in this situation she will know to raise her hand over the man's shoulder to release from the embrace.

The Woman's Left Hand on the Man's Forearm

Some women sometimes put their hand on the man's right forearm. This is never an acceptable closed position. The woman should not make this connection.

The Woman's Left Hand on the Man's Bicep

Some women sometimes put their hand on the man's arm in the area around the man's bicep. This is a bad area to make a connection. First of all, this connection misses the point of closed position, which is to connect with the man's body, not his arm. The man is in closed position, but the woman is in an open position. The more severe problem is that even the most experienced women are not able to dance without at some point using the man's arm to stabilize themselves. When the woman struggles with her balance, she may hang onto the man's arm. Or she may apply pressure to the man's arm for another reason. In any case, she turns the man's shoulder joint into a mortar and pestle. Any man with a shoulder injury will soon find his shoulder inflamed. This is an unsafe position for the man. Therefore the woman's hand on the man's bicep is not a social dance position. A woman should not use this position without permission from her man beforehand. This position is problematic for leading, following, and breaking the connection as well.

The Woman's Left Hand Behind the Man's Arm, on Top of his Shoulder, or Around his Neck

The woman may place her hand behind the man's shoulder, on top of his shoulder, or around his neck, provided she can do so without putting pressure on the man. These positions are problematic for leading, following, and breaking the connection so she needs to have the experience to know what to do.

The Woman's Left Hand Underneath the Man's Right Arm on his Side or Back

Due to height differences, for comfort, or due to injury, the woman may place her left hand underneath the man's right arm, on the man's right side, or around his back. This is a safe position for both partners. You still have the issue of being problematic for leading, following, and releasing from closed position.

Points To Remember

1. The woman's left hand is on the front of the man's right shoulder.

2. The man should lead the same regardless of where the woman made the connection with the man.

3. When the woman's left hand is not on the front of the man's shoulder, the woman needs to dance as if her hand was in the standard position.

4. The woman should not put her left hand on the man's forearm.

5. The woman should not put her left hand on the man's bicep without his permission.

6. The woman may put her hand in another safe position, though the position may be problematic for leading, following, and releasing from closed position.

Counterbalancing

> A dip is when you lower the lady while she supports her own weight. A drop is when you lower the lady while you support some of her weight. ~ Swing dance teacher

This book does not address techniques for doing off-balance tricks other than these notes. If you are going to do these things, you should practice them beforehand.

If you are going to counterbalance, the amount of weight shared should be at the discretion of the woman. On average, the man is bigger than the woman. The woman is usually the one who is more off-balance. The woman is typically more at risk of falling.

When beginning a movement that has the potential for shared weight, start by both people maintaining their own weight fully. The man initiates the movement but the woman initiates the sharing of weight by counterbalancing rather than stepping. Allow the woman to increase the sharing of weight to the level to which she is comfortable. If the man feels like he cannot maintain the woman's weight, he should drop her to save himself. With this last consideration, the woman would be wise to test her partner's ability beforehand.

At the end of the shared weight movement, both partners should be stable, each maintaining their own balance, before attempting some other movement. You should not, for example, from a counterbalanced contra swing, sling the woman into a spin. Stop the swing first. Make sure you are both balanced individually before giving her a turn.

You cannot unambiguously lead a woman into counterbalancing. Counterbalancing is taking your weight in a particular direction without stepping in that direction. The signal for the woman to counterbalance is the same as the signal for her to step in that direction. For the woman to counterbalance, she has to ignore the signal to step. Counterbalancing requires the woman to be off-balance, relying on her man for support. Therefore, you have to make up beforehand what signals you are going to use to indicate you should counterbalance, rather than step.

Once you are counterbalancing, you can no longer communicate unambiguously. You should not try to do much while sharing weight. You need to be careful because there is a present danger of injury.

Points To Remember

1. If you want to counterbalance, practice with your partner beforehand.

Dance As If

You own everything on your side of the connection.

The rules in this book allow you to dance with a partner while meeting the ten values under A for Attitude. There are times when you may choose to deviate from the rules to express yourself. You may do so without your partner's permission, as long as you dance as if you are following the rules so as not to adversely affect your partner.

You should not deviate from a rule until you have mastered the ability to execute the rule. If you deviate from a rule out of inexperience that is a mistake for which your partner will need to compensate. Every person makes mistakes. Mistakes are a normal part of social dancing. Mistakes are not wrong. They are expected. In this discussion, we are talking about the consequences of deviating intentionally, not out of lack of skill.

When you deviate from a rule, you should not affect your partner. If you are going to deviate in a way that affects your partner, you should ask your partner's permission first. One example, previously discussed, is if the woman wants to put her hand in a closed position somewhere other than the front of the man's shoulder.

When you deviate from a rule, you do not need to ask your partner's permission, if you can dance as if you were following the rules. You are free to dance however you like as long as the result, as far as your partner is concerned, is the same. For example, when the man asks the woman to go straight and turn, the man then waits for the woman to finish. The woman's rule is to stay on her line. She is to take every step on the line in the direction indicated. Since the man is waiting for her, as long as she ends up in the right place at the end, she can move on and off the line, go forward and back, or do whatever she feels like. She is still following what she was invited to do.

Be aware that when you deviate you may feel something different. You must be experienced enough to know what to do. For example, the woman's rule is to maintain her frame when the man moves the connection horizontally. By maintaining her frame, the woman begins to step or begins to rotate. This gives the woman the signal for the basic patterns go straight and turn. As long as the woman can respond appropriately, that is do the requested basic patterns, she may choose at times not to maintain her frame.

When you deviate from the rules, you may be in a different position from normal. As long as you can respond to your partner without affecting your partner, you can alter your position. For example, at the end of going straight and turning, your normal final position may be facing your partner. You may choose to end facing diagonally towards your partner. This is fine as long as you can dance as if you were in your normal position.

Points To Remember

1. If you have not mastered the rules, follow them until you can do them consistently.

2. You can deviate from the rules as long as you have the experience to dance as if you are following the rules.

3. When you deviate from the rules, you should not affect your partner.

4. If you want to deviate from the rules in a way that is going to affect your partner, ask your partner first.

Dance Class

> Do not talk. People come to dance class to dance. They do not want to listen to you talking. ~ Edith Weitzen, social dancer and my mother

Debrief After Class

During class, talk to your partner about anything except what you are doing. If you want to discuss your dancing, bring that up with the teacher. If you want, get together after class to debrief.

Dance While the Music Is On

When you go to a dance social, you have to make things work with the way your partner is dancing at that moment. You are not going to fix your partner, or yourself, at a dance social. You have to figure out what you can do, not what your partner can do, to keep dancing. While you are in class, you should practice the same way that you dance at a social. When your teacher puts on music for you to practice, dance, do not talk. You have limited class time to practice. Even if you are confused, keep moving while the music is on.

Exercise First, Explanation Second

> I taught a three-hour workshop in Chicago. Before each exercise, I explained why we were doing the exercise. At the end of the workshop, everyone was worn out.

> One week later, I taught the same workshop. The only difference was first we did the exercise. After the exercise, I explained why we did what we did. At the end of that workshop, nobody wanted to leave. They wanted more.

If you are teaching a dance class, find exercises that illustrate the point you want your students to get. Your students learn better by doing than by explanations. Do not answer questions before they have been asked. Your students will not know what you are talking about. Wait for the students to have questions before you answer them. That way, the students will pay attention to the answers.

Most of Dance Class Should Be Dancing

One dance class I went to regularly was two hours long. The teachers lectured, demonstrated, and would have us do exercises for the two hours. Sometimes they put on a song or two at the end. We might do one or two dances each week, maybe four to eight dances a month. After six months we might have gotten in 24 to 48 dances.

In the classes I run, there is about 15 minutes of instruction spread over each hour. The other 45 minutes is dancing. Songs are about three minutes long. The students do about 15 dances per hour or 30 dances per night. After a month they have done about 120 dances. After 6 months they have done 720 dances.

Who do you think got better faster, and who do you think had more fun, the students doing 48 dances or the students doing 720 dances?

People get better by dancing. People have limited time to devote to their dancing. Often, the one or two dance classes they take a week, are all the opportunity they have to practice. If your students are not dancing on the weekend, allow for practice during your classes. That may be the only time they practice.

Points To Remember

1. Debrief after class.

Dance Class

2. Dance while the music is on.

3. Find exercises that teach, rather than explanations, so students learn by doing.

4. Answer questions after they are asked, not before.

5. Most of the dance class should be dancing.

Do Not Tell Others What To Do

Hi Andy,

I hope that you are having a nice weekend :) I wanted to touch base regarding tango class on Thursday. I left feeling uncomfortable and hurt after my dancing experience with Terry. I imagine that he wanted to help; yet, in the moment I felt criticized, self-conscious, and somatically triggered. I can take ownership of my reactions, yet at the same time, it was my impression that this was a beginner's class that was free of judgement. In that exchange, I did not feel supported, and I do not feel comfortable dancing with him again. Is Terry planning to return to the remaining dance classes? To be honest with you, I am feeling hesitant about returning to class after this experience. I look forward to hearing your thoughts.

Best, Zoe

You should not tell other people what to do.

When You Tell Other People What To Do, They Quit

I am not dancing because I cannot keep the rhythm, and I suck, and have anxiety about it. The last time I went, twice guys changed their spot in line so they were not my partner. ~ Patty, beginning dancer

The worst consequence of telling people what to do is they quit because they feel bad. Try to make people feel good. Learn to enjoy others for the way they are. That will make you a better social dancer than any other skill you can acquire.

Everyone Can Dance

> I will dance with anyone. I social dance for fun. I do not care how good someone is. I have just as much fun with a beginner as with someone who knows what they are doing.

Everyone can dance as long as their partner is willing to dance with them the way they are. If you do not have the skill to have fun dancing with someone the way they are, do not dance with them.

Nobody Is Perfect

If you are going to tell people what to do, when does your criticism stop? Nobody is perfect. Everyone can get better. If your reason for telling someone what to do is to help them get better, then there is no end to your badgering.

Tell the Teacher, Not Your Partner

If you think someone needs some kind of instruction, tell the teacher. There is nothing wrong with you passing your observations along to your teacher.

Telling People What To Do Does Not Work

> While I was teaching a couple a private lesson in swing dancing, Yaw came in. Yaw said to me, "He is stepping back too far. He needs to take a shorter rock-step."
>
> I replied, "I know. I have been telling him that for three weeks."

A person cannot change what they are doing just because you said so. Dancing is a skill that requires muscle memory. To acquire a skill takes practice. Your partner needs to practice for hours to change. If your partner is attending dance class once a week, changing might take months or even years. Your partner is not doing what you think is wrong because your partner does not know what to do. Your partner is doing what they are doing because that is what they can do at that time.

Leave the Instruction to the Teacher

Although almost everyone is nice to the others in class, a friendly reminder: please do not be critical of your partner in class, meaning telling them all is their fault if something did not work. After all, they are there for you to practice your tango.

It is easy to provide criticism but not easy to take it. Let the instructor do the dirty job, pointing out the errors, and provide solutions to repair. ~ Andrea Pham, Argentine tango instructor

You do not think you know more than the teacher, do you? Your teacher knows what to tell your partner better than you do. If you are having a problem with your partner, ask the teacher for help. If someone asks you a question, refer them to the teacher, even if you think you know the answer.

People Want To Hear From the Instructor

I paid $35 to take a class from professional Argentine tango teachers. We rotated so that we danced with four people during the hour and a half class. My first rotation was with the teacher, which was good. The next three people spent the time I was with them telling me what to do, instead of practicing what the teacher taught.

People paid money to take a class from the instructor. They want to hear from the instructor, not you. If you want to discuss what to do with your partner, debrief after class.

Do Not Hijack Someone Else's Class

> Do not hijack someone else's class for your agenda. If you want to tell people what to do, offer your own class. Those that want to hear from you will take your class. ~ Erin King, recreational dancer

The teacher has an agenda for the class. If the teacher feels your partner needs particular instruction, the teacher will instruct your partner. Do not hijack someone else's class to impose your agenda on your partner.

You Interrupt Their Development

> When I am teaching people, I am cautious about telling them what to do. Each person is unique. In my head, I make an assessment for each individual about how they are developing. The most important part of that assessment is their emotional state.

Dancing consists of a myriad of skills. You could list a hundred things for a person to work on. Each person learns different things in their own way at different times, much of which is happening subconsciously. When you tell someone what to do, you interrupt their natural development. For example, suppose a person is learning to keep the rhythm of a dance in time to the music. Learning to keep the rhythm is a complex process. The brain is listening for cues in the music to coordinate with movement. If you tell a person to adjust their posture or have a firmer frame, you interrupted their learning to keep the rhythm. The point is you do not know what is going on inside another person. You do not know how that person is developing. If you are not that person's teacher, you are not responsible for that person's development. Do not take on that responsibility uninvited. Let people learn in their own way.

People Get Better With Time

> As long as my dance students are doing something which is going to lead them to get better, I do not bother them.

Many things that people are doing get better with time. For those things, the person needs experience, not correction. The way to see that people progress is to help them feel good about what they are doing so they want to dance more.

You Are Wrong

> I was dancing with my regular partner. During one dance, she said there was a hold after a particular step. Sometime later, the choreographer was there. He did the dance the way I did the dance without the hold.

In my experience, when someone other than the teacher tells someone what to do, much of the time they are wrong. Even though you think you know what you are doing, consider that you are more likely to be wrong than right. Even when you are right, you are wrong. For example, you may be observing something your partner is doing that is wrong. However, your partner may be doing the wrong thing because you are doing something wrong. You may call the teacher over only to have the teacher correct you instead of your partner. You may have been correct that your partner was doing something wrong, but your teacher may have felt in this instance that you would benefit from the correction rather than your partner. Another example is you are correct that your partner is doing something wrong, but what you tell them is wrong. Suppose your partner has no frame. You tell your partner to firm up their frame, or horribly, you tell them to push to keep their frame firm. Now you have taught them some bad habits.

You Create a Problem for the Other Person

Do not say, "Can I give you some feedback?" You put the other person in an awkward position. When you tell someone what to do, you create a problem for that person. That person has to stop what they are doing to do what you say. Otherwise, they have a conflict with you. Consider what options you have left for the other person. They can refuse to do what you told them. They can argue with you. Or they can give in. None of these options are good for them. Most people are conflict-averse so they give in.

You Create the Wrong Relationship

When you tell someone what to do, you create the wrong relationship. You created a hierarchy where you are the dominant partner judging the other person. The other person has to be cautious about what they are doing or suffer more of your criticism. You have just blocked that person from dancing freely. Is that what you want? Do you want to limit your partner to only dance your way? Do you only want to enjoy experiences you control? This is not fair to your partner. You miss out on the variety you had a chance to experience.

You Are Complaining, Not Helping

A student came to me with a complaint about his partner. He said she was tight, took too small steps, and needed to loosen up. He said this took away from the enjoyment of the dance.

I told him I knew. I would continue to work with her. Maybe in the long term, she would open up. However, the best thing for him to do was to learn to enjoy dancing with her the way she dances now. I do.

By now you should understand when you tell someone else what to do in someone else's class or at social dancing, you are not helping, you are criticizing. When you keep criticizing, your criticism turns into complaining. Your complaints may be correct observations, but they do no good. Work on yourself, not others.

Do Not Ask Your Partner What To Do

You may think asking your partner what to do is alright even if the teacher told you not to. Asking your partner does more harm with little good. If your partner buys into the teacher's method, your partner will tell you to ask the teacher. Your asking your partner then is a discourtesy to your partner. Your partner will only answer you if your partner does not buy into your teacher's method. In that case, your partner is giving you misinformation relative to your teacher's method. When the teacher puts on the music, you interrupt that limited practice time by talking with your partner. Not only did you lose the time, you lost the continuity of dancing through an entire song. You caused your partner to lose out as well. Consider that your teacher wants you to figure things out for yourself. Your teacher knows what problems you are going to experience. Your teacher is waiting for you to ask the appropriate questions so you will be ready to receive the answers. If you ask your partner instead of the teacher, you do not get the answers.

Little by Little

I was at SeaWorld where a trainer was explaining how they got a whale to jump out of the water over a rope. Aside from the morality of holding an orca in captivity, the process is enlightening. They put a rope on the bottom of the pool. When the whale swims over the rope, they give the whale a fish. At some point, the whale figures out he gets a fish when he swims over the rope. Then they raise the rope off the bottom. Eventually, the whale has to breach the surface to go over the rope to get the fish. Finally, the whale has to jump clear out of the water to get over the rope for the fish reward.

Improvement takes time. People get better little by little. Have patience. Understanding is what people need to improve at social dancing.

Become a Teacher

A new woman came to our ballroom class. She was doing something the teacher had said, but not what I was leading. I told her she should try to follow me. She walked off the floor instead. I was the worst about telling people what to do, so I became a teacher.

If you want to tell people what to do, start your own class. People that want to hear your instruction will attend your class. Once you are a teacher, you will learn to value your own instruction. If people ask you outside of your class for instruction, you will tell them to come to your class.

Points To Remember

1. When you tell people what to do, they quit.

2. Telling people what to do does not work.

3. Leave the instruction for the teacher.

4. People paid to hear from the instructor, not you.

5. Do not hijack someone else's class for your agenda.

6. You interrupt the other person's development.

7. People get better with time without your instruction.

8. You are wrong.

9. You create a problem for the other person.

10. You create the wrong relationship.

11. You are complaining, not helping.

12. Do not ask your partner what to do.

13. Have patience.

14. If you want to tell people what to do, start your own class.

Geometry, Not Physics

How do I know where to go? Follow the rules.

The method of communicating in this book uses geometry, not physics. This book uses position and direction to communicate, which are geometry. The method does not use force and momentum, which are physics. Below, the author lists the geometric elements of the communication system. The author leaves to the reader the exercise of defining the elements of a force-based communication system.

The Connection

This book uses geometry to define the connection. The connection is defined by the points that are touching your partner.

The Stationary Position of the Follower

The man defines the stationary position of the woman by where he places the connection. Geometrically, there is only one place the woman can be to maintain the connection.

Where To Move

This book uses geometry to define where the woman is to move. The man moves the connection in the direction he wants the woman to go. He moves the connection to indicate the three directions of straight, turn, and circle. This creates an arrow initiating the direction of movement.

Four Basic Patterns

The direction signals indicate to the woman to do four geometric, basic patterns go straight on a line, turn in place, walk around in a circle, and turn while traveling on a line or circle.

When the Woman Stops

When the woman is to stop is defined geometrically. The woman stops moving when the man blocks her direction of movement, or when she reaches the end of her connection.

Force

Force is physics. As noted many times, you should not use force.

Momentum

Momentum is physics. Momentum propels you in the direction you are moving. You should not use momentum. When you complete a step, you should be balanced so you can stop. You should be able to proceed in any direction. You should not let your momentum carry you past your step. Ideally, you should be able to stop at any point throughout your step.

Points To Remember

1. The method of communicating in this book uses geometry, not physics.

Insights

I am constantly amazed how the ABCDs continually reveals new insights. I wrote those words in 2008. I first put the three laws on paper in 2007. As I update the book now in 2022, I am still amazed at how the three laws continue to reveal new insights after fifteen years.

The introduction of this book promised the following insights would be explained. They have been explained in the book. Here is a short explanation for each of the items promised. Refer back to the appropriate sections for further discussion. Keep going back to the three laws and ten principles. You will find answers there. You will find new insights. This ability to continue to provide answers reveals how powerful these ideas are. The three laws are at the heart of a deep truth.

Definition of social dancing
Dancing that puts the social nature of dancing first.

Definition of social dance choreography
Any choreography you can unambiguously communicate safely without having practiced with your partner.

Definition of the ten foundational values so you have a clear understanding of what is important for social dancing
Safety, courtesy, comfort, teamwork, natural, freedom, clearly defined, easy, fast, and universal

Definition of the three laws that let you communicate every step unambiguously
Law of balance: everyone maintains their own balance. Law of connection: the woman maintains the connection. Law of direction: the woman maintains her direction.

Three signals that let you communicate every figure

Straight, turn, and circle.

Definition of the man's responsibilities

Keep time with the music. Position the couple on the dance floor. Initiate the woman's movement.

Definition of the woman's responsibilities

Keep time with the man. Maintain the connection. Complete her movement.

Definition of signals relative to horizontal and vertical movement so you know where to move

Horizontal only movement of the connection signals the woman's horizontal movement. The three horizontal signals are straight, turn, and circle. Any vertical movement of the connection vertically adjusts the woman's arms or body without moving her horizontal position.

Definition of woman's line of dance so the woman can dance with precision

When the man moves the connection horizontally, the woman initiates her step, creating an imaginary line on the floor called the woman's line of dance. To complete her choreography, the woman takes every step on her line.

Definition of the three positions

Free position is when the partners are not physically touching. Open position is when the partners are touching, but not in an embrace. Closed position is when the partners are in an embrace.

Examination of balance so you understand why balance is the most important skill in dancing

To move as one with your partner, you need to control your movement throughout your step. You control your step via balance.

Examination of pressure and tension so you understand why you should not push and pull on your partner

Pushing and pulling violate all ten values and the three laws.

Examination of the two types of horizontal movement so you understand why every step can be communicated unambiguously

There are only two types of horizontal movement: (1) step and (2) rotate.

Explanation of the four basic patterns that make up every figure in the woman's choreography

The four basic patterns are: (1) go straight, (2) turn in place, (3) walk around in a circle, and (4) turn while traveling.

Explanation of why the man can communicate the woman's choreography

The man can communicate the woman's choreography while doing his own choreography because the woman's choreography is defined by the simple system in this book. All the woman's choreography is comprised of the four basic patterns.

Explanation of why the woman cannot communicate the man's choreography

The woman cannot communicate the man's choreography while doing her own choreography because the man's choreography is too complex to define in a simple system. While the woman is doing her four basic patterns, the man may be doing far more complex maneuvers.

Guidelines for navigating the dance floor to improve safety

See the section on safety.

Guidelines for etiquette in the social dance setting to make your group more respectful

See the section on courtesy.

How to communicate unambiguously without using visual clues

Follow the laws of balance, connection, and direction.

How to communicate unambiguously visually when not physically connected

The woman maintains an imaginary physical connection midway between the partners. The woman mirrors the man.

How to communicate unambiguously in choreographed dances

Follow the laws of balance, connection, and direction.

How to communicate rhythm changes

The man moves the connection to communicate changes of rhythm.

How to step for effective communication

Posture, feet together, walk on a line underneath your body, move from your center, engage your rear end, place your free foot, push with your supporting leg, transfer your weight, bring your knees and ankles together, collect your feet, complete your step.

Rules for connecting and breaking the connection

The man chooses when to make and break the connection. In free position, the man breaks or makes the visual connection by some obvious action. In open position, the man makes or breaks the physical connection, or the man makes a presentation of connection inviting the woman to connect. In closed position, the man connects with the woman in an embrace. The woman closes the embrace by connecting with the man's body. When the man breaks the embrace, the woman releases the body connection.

Rules for the woman's choreography

The woman's choreography is go straight, turn in place, walk in a circle, or turn while traveling.

Rules for when the woman follows the man

Insights

The woman follows the man at all times.

Rules for when the woman is to maintain and adjust her frame
The woman maintains her frame when the connection moves horizontally only. Otherwise, she allows her frame to adjust.

Rules of when the woman stops her motion
The woman stops her motion when she reaches the end of her connection or her movement is blocked.

Rules for when the man waits for the woman
The man waits for the woman after he initiates her choreography.

Rules for not getting your foot stepped on
Whoever is going backwards is responsible for not getting their foot stepped on and for not bumping knees.

Points To Remember

1. Keep going back to the three laws and ten principles to find answers.

2. The ten foundational values are safety, courtesy, comfort, teamwork, natural, freedom, clearly defined, easy, fast, and universal

3. Law of Balance: everyone maintains their own balance.

4. Law of Connection: the woman maintains the connection.

5. Law of Direction: the woman maintains her direction.

Man's Movement

Where the man goes has nothing to do with you.

You only need to know how the man communicates what the woman is to do. The man's choreography is not relevant to the communication.

The structure of choreography allows the man to communicate every step to the woman unambiguously in time to the music. The reason this is possible is the woman makes only three movements, straight, turn, and circle. The woman's movements can be defined with a simple method, as described in this book. The reverse is not true. The man makes more complex movements than the woman. The man's choreography cannot be communicated unambiguously using a simple system.

For example, say the man and woman start facing each other in an open position. In a simple pass, the man invites the woman to go straight and make a half turn to face back where she started. The man can execute this in any number of ways. Let us take a simple way. The man steps back to his right out of the woman's way, making a quarter turn to face the woman's line of dance. After the woman passes, he steps back on the woman's line, making another quarter turn to face the woman. The couple end facing each other with the man staying in the center. The woman has gone from one side to the other side of the man. How could the woman unambiguously communicate the man's choreography while she is doing her own steps? I cannot think of a simple method.

The problem runs deeper. To execute various movements the man has to alter his timing, stepping either before or after the woman. Often the man has to change the shape of his frame. There are other considerations as well. The complexity is too much to communicate.

Points To Remember

1. The man's choreography is too complex to define with a simple system.

Method Name

Let us know your suggestions for name for the method described in this book. Please note, only send us suggestions to which you relinquish all rights.

In version 0.93 the author removed all references to a method name. The reason being the difficulty of finding a method name that can be trademarked.

The name of the method described in this book in version 0.92 was Harmony^{SM} along with Harmony Dancer^{SM}.

The method described in this book needs a name for people to refer to the method in their communication with one another. A group may want to let people know that they practice the method in this book. This indicates to visitors the characteristics that come with the method, such as no use of force and an explicit method of communicating choreography.

The original name of the method, coined in 2007, was Partnership Dancing. An appeal court of judges at the US Patent and Trademark Office (USPTO) ruled that Partnership Dancing was merely descriptive, equating the meaning of the word partnership with the word partner, therefore not admissible for trademark. I argued that the word partnership was like the word corporation, arguing that Partnership Dancing, like Corporation Dancing, was meaningless in the context of social dancing. The judges rejected my argument that words have definite meanings, refusing to acknowledge the dictionary definition of partnership, which does not mean partner any more than battleship means battle. I learned that judges can attribute meanings to words without regard to dictionary definitions. If judges ignore dictionary definitions of words, then laws can mean whatever judges feel like with wide latitude.

Trademarks and service marks are important to identify to the public that you are getting what you think you are getting. If you see a sign that says we teach Harmony^{SM} here, you want to know you are getting the real thing. The service mark symbol next to Harmony^{SM} is a legal notice. No one may use this name without the consent of the service mark owner. The trademark or service mark symbol only needs to appear prominently once somewhere at the beginning of the document. The symbol does not need to appear every time the trademark or service mark words are used.

The USPTO has a habit of rejecting trademarks and service marks as merely descriptive, which is why so many people use their name in the trademark and service mark. If the USPTO rejects this service mark as merely descriptive, the method name may become Andrew Weitzen's Harmony℠ or something similar.

When this book was readable only on my website, I was able to program the name of the method into the book. This allowed for easily changing the method name. However, as this version is intended for distribution on other platforms, and since the method name has not been registered with the USPTO, the method name may need to be changed in the future. To avoid extensive editing, I have avoided using the method name throughout the book, instead referring to the method described in this book.

Points To Remember

1. Send us your suggestions for a name for the method.

2. Only send us suggestions to which you relinquish all rights.

3. In version 0.92, the name of the method described in this book was Harmony℠ along with Harmony Dancer℠.

4. The original method name in 2007 was Partnership Dancing℠ along with Partnership Dancer℠..

Mixers and Changing Partners

Stay put when left where you are. Go when sent.

The rules for changing partners during a dance are the same as dancing with a single partner. You can change partners using the method in this book. The man and woman follow the rules they normally follow. These notes help clarify the transition from one partner to another.

The Woman Waits Where She Is

One way the man releases his partner is by breaking the connection, leaving her where she is with no motion. The woman who is left without motion should dance in place until a man picks her up.

The Woman Continues in Her Motion

The second way the man releases his partner is by asking her to go in a particular direction then breaking the connection. The woman continues in her direction as she normally would until she is picked up by another man.

Connecting in Closed Position With a New Partner

To pick up a new partner in closed position, the man puts his right hand on the woman's left shoulder blade. The woman follows the rule under connection to close the position. She now has a new partner.

Connecting in Open Position With a New Partner

To pick up a new partner in open position, the man presents the connection to the woman or joins with the woman by making the connection himself.

Cutting in to Steal a Partner

Either a man or a woman can cut in to take away someone else's partner, providing this is permitted by the group's social etiquette, such as in a birthday dance jam circle. For either a man or woman to cut in in open position, follow the above procedure for connecting in open position. The new partner can step in between the partners when there is room.

For a man to cut in in closed position, the man follows the above procedure for connecting in closed position, by placing his hand on the shoulder blade of the new partner. For a woman to cut in in closed position, she places her left hand on the man's right shoulder. The man releases his current partner and connects with his new partner. This is a special signal for a mixer when the etiquette permits a woman to cut in.

Points To Remember

1. When changing partners in dances, the same rules apply.

2. A woman can cut in by placing her left hand on the man's right shoulder.

Musicality

> The dance has to fit the music. ~ Yoav Ashriel, Israeli folk dance choreographer

Dance to the Music

What is dancing? Dancing is your rhythmic expression of music. The better you understand the music, the more opportunities you have for interpretation. Music has structure. Listen for this structure to express your dancing to the music. Following is a discussion of the typical structure of popular, dance music. Music does not have to conform to this structure.

Time Signature

The basic unit of music is the note. The note is divided into parts, which we call beats. Music is written in a time signature. The time signature describes the number of beats per measure of music. The time signature looks like a fraction with a top and bottom number. The bottom number is the length of the beat. When the bottom number is a four that means there are four beats to a note. The length of a beat is a quarter note. The top number is the number of beats per measure. If the top number is also a four, that means there are four quarter notes to a measure of music. Much social dance music is written in 2/4, 3/4, or 4/4 time, meaning two, three, or four quarter notes per measure.

> 2/4 - Merengue, Samba
> 3/4 – Waltz
> 4/4 – Cha-Cha, Swing

Musical Phrase

Two measures of music make up a musical phrase. The musical phrase corresponds to a line in the song. The two measures have the same rhythm but often are not identical. Through accents, you can hear the difference between the first measure and the second.

Structure of a Song

We dance to songs that often have lyrics in the form of a poem that tells a story. Authors write lyrics in phrases. A series of phrases make up a verse, often four phrases to a verse. A number of verses make up the song. Often a chorus repeats after a couple of verses. Before the song starts, typically there is an introduction. The structure of the parts of a song may be Introduction, ABC, ABC, and ABC. Listen to the music. Understand the structure.

--- Song ---
Introduction

Verse A
Verse B
Chorus

Verse A
Verse B
Chorus

Verse A
Verse B
Chorus

Rhythm

The phrases in the poem have a cadence. Remember iambic pentameter from high school Shakespeare classes? The composer put a musical backdrop to the song to match the cadence, which is called the rhythm. Various instruments make up the rhythm section of the band, typically percussion and bass. The basic rhythm repeats throughout the song. This basic rhythm makes up the rhythm of the dance. A song may have more than one underlying rhythm played one on top of the other. You can dance to whatever rhythm moves you.

Basic Steps

Each dance has a basic set of steps that correspond to the rhythm of the dance. When you step, you should step in time to the beat of the music. When your basic set of steps exactly fit a measure of music, you should correspond your stepping to the measure. When your basic set of steps fit a musical phrase, you should correspond your stepping to the phrase.

Counting

Counting the beats helps you keep time with the music. Any counting system that works for you is good. Counting is a tool. Counting is not dancing.

You should count. When you hear unfamiliar music, you may have trouble hearing the beat. You may see others that hear the beat clearly. Your ears are picking up the same sounds, but your brain is not. When you count, you give your brain a clue as to what to listen for in the music.

One way to count is to count each beat as a number. You start over as the musical pattern repeats. You should count in time to the music. Each word you say corresponds to a step. So if the music was a four-beat repeating pattern, you could count One, Two, Three, Four, indicating you were taking a step on each beat.

When you step on every beat that is like marching. One way dancing differs from marching is you can alter the timing of your steps in dancing. You can add extra steps between beats or pause to wait for beats to pass. By altering the timing of your steps, you add variety to the dance.

In the numeric counting system, you can use the word "and" to add a step around halfway between beats. You might count swing as One, Two, Three And Four, Five, Six, Seven And Eight, which would indicate that you are taking an extra step about halfway between three and four of each measure.

To step near the beat you can use the word "a". You might count hustle as a-One, Two, Three, a-One, Two, Three, to indicate that you are taking an extra step near the beat before one.

To skip a beat, you leave out the number. You might count salsa as One, Two, Three, while remaining quiet on four to indicate that you are not stepping on four. Or you can use the word "Hold" as in One, Two, Three, Hold-Four,

Another way to count is to use the words "Slow" and "Quick". A "Quick" step is stepping on the beat. One "Slow" indicates a step followed by a pause. Two Quick steps take the same time as one Slow step. A Slow can represent either one or two beats of music, depending on the dance and how fast the music is. You might count rumba as Slow, Quick, Quick. You might count foxtrot as Slow, Slow, Quick, Quick.

Tempo

The tempo is how fast the beats are played. The average speed for dance music is about a half-second per beat with about 120 beats per minute. To be able to dance at different tempos, you have to practice dancing to each specific tempo. If you want to be able to dance to slow music or fast music, you have to practice dancing to slow music and fast music. To feel comfortable dancing to slow music, you can elongate your steps. You can add rising and falling on certain steps for some dances. To feel comfortable dancing to fast music, you can shorten your steps. As you would expect, the basic footwork for slow music often has more steps, while the basic footwork for fast music often has fewer steps. How slow or fast a dance feels is the combination of the number of steps you take relative to how fast the music is. The type of step also affects your speed. Partial steps in which you do not fully transfer your body over your supporting foot, are faster than full steps.

Step on the Beat

> In a documentary about Gene Kelly, the narrator talked about the athleticism with which Kelly danced. He said the power in Kelly's dancing came from Kelly leading the music. A world champion couple said in rumba their secret was to arrive with their weight exactly on the beat. Another dance teacher said in hustle she liked to finish transferring her weight after the beat.

You should step on the beat of the music, but what exactly does that mean? Each style of dance may have different criteria for when your foot strikes the floor and when your body arrives over your foot. Should your foot strike the floor on the beat or should your body arrive over your foot on the beat? Exactly when to transfer your weight is up to your musical interpretation.

Similarly, how you move from one step to another is open to your musical interpretation. Intermediate dancers typically move at a steady pace. If the music is slow, they move slowly. If the music is fast, they rush. Advanced dancers alter how they move to express themselves to the music. If the music is slow, an advanced dancer may delay their step momentarily then explode into their step, as one example. Both the intermediate and advanced dancers are keeping the same beat. The intermediate dancer is marching. The advanced dancer is interpreting the music.

Synchronize Basic Steps With the One Beat in the Phrase

> In our beginning swing dancing class, Richard told me one of the guys was not doing the 6-count basic steps. I told Richard, "I know. He hears the music well. He instinctively adds two extra steps so that he starts each figure on the one in the musical phrase."

You should start dancing on the first beat of the first verse after the introduction. Ideally, throughout the dance, you should synchronize your first step of a movement with the first beat in a phrase of the music. When the number of beats in a measure does not correspond evenly to the number of steps in a basic pattern, you need multiple measures of music to get back to your starting foot being free on the one count of the music.

Waltz has three beats per measure, but you need six steps to return to your starting position. You should wait for the one beat in the six-count phrase to start your waltz. Otherwise, you will feel the emphasis in your dancing is not coordinated with the music.

Swing has typical six and eight-count movements, although you can improvise movements of any length. You should start eight-count movements on the one in an eight-count phrase because they exactly match the music. You need to do four six-count movements in a row to get back to matching the one count in the musical phrase.

Some songs have an extra measure between verses. For example, in some waltzes, after some verses, there are an extra three beats of music. If you dance on the beat throughout the song, at some point you will be on the opposite foot on the one beat of the music. When you pass another transition, you will be back onto your original foot on the one. If you have the skill, when you hear the transition, instead of stepping on all the beats, you can pause on a beat so that you stay on your original foot on the one.

Melody

On top of the repeating rhythm is a melody. The melody corresponds to the words of the song. The singer carries the melody assisted by instruments in the band. While the rhythm is steady, the melody can speed up, slow down, stretch, and compress. You can use the melody to alter the basic rhythm of a dance. Listen for the structure in the melody. One structure is a call and response. In one phrase, the melody seems to call out. In the following phrase, the melody seems to answer. This is one way the music interacts with you. Unlike only listening to music, one of the wonders of dancing is you can interact with the music. Enrich your experience by connecting your dancing to the melody.

Musical Tension

Songs are written in a particular key. A key is a base note on the musical scale around which the music plays. Sometimes, the music moves away from the base note, possibly stair-stepping higher or changing to another key temporarily. This creates emotional tension in you because you feel the music needs to return to the natural state for that song. Typically the music resolves the musical tension by moving back to the base key, often in a dramatic fashion depending on the musical style. Listen for the creation of musical tension. Be prepared for the resolution so you can add styling to your dancing at this dramatic moment.

The tension is not random. The tension is created through a musical progression of chords or other means, which is generally consistent throughout a song. Your brain becomes conditioned for a specific type of progression based on the type of music for that particular song. Tension is expressed in verses that are made up of the phrases of the music. The number of phrases in a verse is characteristic of the type of music. Swing music typically has 4 phrases of eight beats. Blues music has 6 phrases of eight beats. You can hear the difference in each phrase as the musical tension is increased. At the end, you can hear the music resolve back to the base scale.

Musical Breaks

There can be breaks in the music when the singer or the instruments stop. Breaks can be abrupt or can simply be fading. Depending on the dance, you might pause your dancing during a break. You may be having a hard time figuring out how to add some type of musicality to your dancing. One of the easiest ways is to simply stop dancing during breaks in the music. Resume dancing when the music starts again. To add musicality to your dancing, you have to do something physical. Once you start adding some physical alteration to your dancing, you put yourself on the path to grow your musical expression.

Jams With Shines

Kind of the opposite of a break is when the musicians jam out. They get away from the verses of the song. The singer may stop singing with only music playing. The music may lose the differences between phrases. There may be no more verses for a while. Sometimes the musicians might jam for as long as a minute in the middle of a song. This can be difficult to dance to with a partner. This is a good time to break away from your partner to do shines. Shines are when you do fancy steps on your own. During the jamming, you can let go of your partner. You dance on your own for a while. When you hear the jam ending, you pick your partner back up. Or you can do what I do, which is cut the jams out of the music before playing.

Match Your Dancing to the Melody, Breaks, and Tension

Once you can match your dancing to the phrases in the music, you can take your inspiration to the next level. Listen to the elements of the song. Match your dancing to what you hear. During the verse of the song, you might do more creative dancing. During the chorus, you might vary your style. During musical breaks, you might stop altogether. During the resolution of musical tension, you might do something dramatic.

Structure Your Choreography to the Song

The leader has the most control to structure the choreography. An example of structuring your choreography to a song is this. During the introduction, you walk your partner into position. You move into a closed position. You relax taking a deep breath to let your partner get comfortable. You step on one foot for a measure then on the other foot for a measure to synchronize. You start to dance on the first note of the first verse. The first time through the song you keep your choreography simple to see what your partner can do. During the chorus, you do something repetitively. During the second time through the song, you do your fancy moves. The last time through the song, you wind down.

Points To Remember

1. Music has structure.

2. Count to the beat of the music.

3. Use the one beat.

4. Match your dancing to the music.

New Dancers

Conchi and James signed up for my beginning swing class. Conchi said, "We go to One Love Café all the time. We dance, but we do not know what we are doing. There is a couple that comes, Al and Claudia, that are wonderful dancers. We wanted to be able to dance together too."

I said, "Al started in this same class. Claudia came to my classes for years."

Here are some tips to help new dancers get started. Print the one-page rules summary. Memorize the ten values. Memorize the three laws. Apply the ideas however they make sense to you. Do not worry about the details for starters. You will have enough trouble keeping the rhythm of the dance you are learning. Most importantly, learn to dance without using force. Next, do not tell anyone else what to do. Try not to develop bad habits. Leaders, do not attempt to control your partners. Followers, follow. Read this book often. Read the sections that are pertinent to what you are learning in class. Use this book as a reference. Read the appropriate sections for answers to your questions.

New dancers need specific guidance not found in this book. Social dancing is challenging for everyone, even experienced dancers. This is one of the reasons why people love social dancing. The challenge can be overwhelming for new dancers. To help you navigate the early stages, see my *Beginner's Guide to Learning Social Dancing* by Andrew Weitzen.

Points To Remember

1. Print and memorize the rules.

2. See my book *Beginners Guide to Learning Social Dancing* by Andrew Weitzen.

Popularizing Partner Dancing

Social partner dancing today is done only by enthusiasts, which is a small percentage of the population. That is a shame because dancing is a wonderful social activity that would offer many advantages if incorporated into our mainstream culture. Some of the advantages that social dancing offers are:

1. A wholesome atmosphere because social dancing can only take place in an atmosphere of respect.

2. Building friendships since people interact with others on a regular basis.

3. Creating community diversity since people interact with people of all ages across all backgrounds.

4. Healthier lifestyle by promoting physical and mental activity.

5. Developing character by building confidence through social skills.

6. Lower alcohol consumption since people cannot partner dance when inebriated.

Social dancing is uplifting to people of all ages, helping people to be emotionally, physically, and intellectually healthy, thereby improving the quality of life. An activity that makes for a better social community makes for a better society. The public should have an interest in promoting social dancing.

One problem is social partner dancing is too hard for most people. Lots of people come to dance classes with the hopes of learning to dance. They soon quit when they see how hard dancing is. Dancing is too hard for two main reasons. First, the footwork is hard. Any type of dancing that requires specific footwork in time to music requires a good deal of training. People that go to dance class only once a week may take a couple of years to start feeling comfortable. People starting out dancing are not ready for that kind of commitment.

The solution to the footwork problem is for newcomers to do dances that do not require footwork. Some dances only ask people to follow directions, such as contra, English, and square dancing. These dances most people can do their first day. They can drop in whenever they have a chance without having to make a commitment to learning to dance. When they are ready to make that weekly commitment, they can start ballroom, salsa, swing, and the like. As a dance community, we should provide opportunities for newcomers to go to contra and similar dances. All the dance groups should encourage their beginners to go contra dancing. This is the best entry point into social dancing. This is a way to keep new dancers connected to the dance community even if they drop out of regular classes. Later on, they may return.

The second problem is the inability to communicate. There is a lack of a consistent protocol. The effort to learn to communicate with some level of proficiency is too great for most people's emotional endurance. Those that do learn find their dance skills are barely transferable within their own class from person to person, let alone to others outside of their class, and hardly at all to another style of dance. People have to learn different methods of communicating for each type of dance they do, sometimes for each teacher they have, and worse, sometimes for each partner. This limits mobility within the dance community with people sticking to one type of dance and favoring regular partners, stunting the growth of communities.

This book offers the solution to the communication problem. The ABCDs are easy to learn. Dancers learn fundamental rules instead of relying on experience so beginners can learn to communicate without having to put in years of training. Communication skills are transferable to every person in every social dance so people only need to learn to communicate once and can apply their skills everywhere. Being clearly defined makes the ABCDs ideal for including in grade school, university, and adult education curriculums. This book offers the easy expansion of partner dancing to other dance forms, such as hip hop, without having to create a syllabus of dance patterns.

Points To Remember

1. Social dancing provides exceptional benefits to individuals and therefore society.

2. Newcomers should be encouraged to go to contra and similar dancing that does not require footwork so they can enjoy dancing right away.

3. Adopting the method in this book overcomes the communication issues making social dancing accessible to more people because it is so easy to learn.

4. The ABCDs are ideal for including in public education to bring the benefits of social dancing to society.

Pressure and Tension

> To get the perfect amount of tension and pressure requires years of practice. Most people never get it. ~ June, West Coast swing dance instructor

In contra dancing, people say giving weight. In ballroom dancing, they tell you to imagine you are holding up a pane of glass between you and your partner. In swing dancing, they say pressure and tension. Even the words pressure and tension are not appealing. Who wants pressure and tension in their dancing? Whatever the euphemism, pushing and pulling on your partner is bad.

New Dancers Do Not Push and Pull

If you are new to dancing, you probably do not have a problem with pressure and tension. I have found new dancers, ones that have never danced before, rarely push and pull. When you stick your hands out, new dancers calmly rest their hands in yours, as they should. New dancers effortlessly learn to use the perfect amount of pressure and tension, which is none. To acquire the bad habit of using pressure and tension, you have to teach a new dancer to push and pull. Sadly, five minutes after they start dancing with others their brains are destroyed from being thrown off balance. Then they are pushing, pulling, and grasping with their fingers to hang on for dear life.

You Do Not Know How To Use Your Balance

If you have been dancing for a while, you may like some tension in the connection. You may think you cannot feel your partner. You may think you need an action and reaction to get moving. The problem is you have not acquired the skill to know how to use your balance. You are not aware of how your partner is balanced. You do not know how to time your movement so that your partner moves naturally in response.

Be a Maestro or a Banger

You may think you like dancing with a little pushing and pulling better than dancing without the use of force. You cannot make that comparison because you have not developed the skill to experience what dancing is like without pushing and pulling. You are like the non-dancer who says they do not like to dance when they do not know how to dance. You are a dancer who is saying you do not like to dance without tension when you do not know how to dance without tension. Everything you do with pushing and pulling you can do better without. If you commit to dancing without using force, you will learn how. If you rely on tugging and nudging your partner about, you will not learn how. You can choose to be a maestro or a banger.

Pressure and Tension Violate All Ten Values and the Three Laws

The problems with pressure and tension are so fundamental that they adversely affect every step of your dance. If something violates just one of the ten values, that something cannot be good. Pressure and tension violate all ten values and the three laws. You need to understand them if you still intend to push and pull.

In the following, we will go through each of the ten values and the three laws to see some of the ways pushing and pulling are inhibiting your dancing. As an exercise for you, try to think of at least one additional way pushing and pulling is bad for each of these ten values and the three laws.

Safety

Pressure and tension are not safe. Pressure and tension affect your balance. When you push and pull on someone you could cause them to lose their balance and fall. You are also putting stress on their joints, particularly their shoulders which is especially bad when turning. This is reason enough to not use pressure and tension, but there are many more.

Courtesy

You want to treat your partners respectfully. You should not push or pull on another person without getting their approval first. In normal social interactions, you would be rude to push or pull another person. If you want someone to do something, such as go outside with you, you do not grab them and drag them outside, that is if you are older than six. The socially acceptable way to get someone to do something is to ask them.

Comfort

Wrestling your partner around the dance floor for hours on end may be a good workout, but you will not be comfortable. You can tell the people that are pushing and pulling the most by the ones that are working up the biggest sweat.

Teamwork

Pressure and tension change the nature of your relationship with your partner. When you apply pressure and tension to your partner, the leader has to drag the follower around. The relationship is no longer one among equals. The leader is now the boss. The follower is subservient. Without pressure and tension, you are teammates.

Natural

Pushing and pulling are not natural. Pressure and tension create unnatural handholds. After a turn, when you use pressure and tension, your arm can bend into an awkward position. Without tension and pressure, you can turn your hand freely so your arm ends in a natural position.

Freedom

Tension and pressure restrict your freedom of movement because you are hanging onto one another. Your ability to express yourself is reduced. Without pressure and tension, you have maximum freedom of movement.

Clearly Defined

Since each person uses a different amount of pressure and tension at different times, you cannot have a clearly defined, precise, logical, unambiguous communication system. The woman cannot know exactly when the man wants her to move. Since you are pushing and pulling on one another, she cannot know whether she should move to another position, or if her current position is correct. When her partner changes the amount of force, she does not know whether to move or to counter his force to remain in the same position.

Easy

Pressure and tension are hard to implement. Pushing and pulling on your partner from all angles is physically difficult, especially while moving. For those people that push and pull, there is an ideal amount of pressure and tension, which takes much experience to master. Your body is not in equilibrium when you use force. At times, different parts of your body are attempting to move in different directions at the same time. You may pull back on your partner while moving forward. In a closed position, you may push back with your shoulder blade, while pushing forward with your hand, all while trying to move somewhere. Force increases the difficulty of your coordination. Moving with a partner is hard enough without the added difficulty of trying to coordinate where to push and pull on your partner with which body part.

Fast

Pressure and tension are slow ways to communicate. When you use pressure and tension, you must take yourself off balance in the opposite direction of the way in which you want to go. You have to recover to the neutral position to do your next movement so you lose time on both ends. To communicate your message, you have to overcome the force the other person is applying. You have to rush through your movements. Without pressure and tension, you have the most time to complete your movements. You can dance relaxed.

Universal

Pressure and tension are not transferable to other people or other dances. Pressure and tension are different from moment to moment, from movement to movement, from dance to dance, even with the same person. With pressure and tension, you have to get used to a regular partner in a particular dance for a particular move. You have to depend on experience. This limits your growth. If you do not use pressure and tension, you only need to learn to communicate once. You can apply the same communication skills to every person in every dance.

Law of Balance

When you use pressure and tension, you apply force to your partner. You violate the law of balance because you can no longer maintain your own balance. You violate the associated principles. You violate the principles that everyone does their own dancing and that everyone moves their own body parts. You throw your partner off-balance when you lead her. You force your leader off-balance when you make him push and pull on you to get you to move.

Law of Connection

When you use pressure and tension, you violate the law of connection. With pressure and tension, you require the leader to maintain the connection in addition to the follower. You limit the type of connections you can make. You limit the angles at which you can make a connection.

Law of Direction

When you use pressure and tension you violate the law of direction. The woman can no longer move freely in the direction she is to go. She must wait to be dragged or pushed through her movement.

Eliminate Pushing and Pulling

As soon as you quit pushing and pulling, you will be compelled to exam how your bodies move in relation to one another. You will learn how to communicate through the natural movement of your bodies. You will force yourself to find ways to improve your dancing.

Points To Remember

1. Pressure and tension are bad for your dancing.

2. New dancers do not push and pull.

3. You have to learn the bad habit of applying force to your partner.

4. Pressure and tension violate all ten values and the three laws.

5. When you eliminate pushing and pulling, you force yourself to find ways to improve your dancing.

Proof

This chapter offers proof of sorts for the method of communicating choreography in social dancing described in this book.

The Problem Is How to Communicate Unambiguously

Some 25 years ago, when taking casino salsa, I started documenting the complex choreography. The problem I was trying to solve was how do women know what to do. In other words, how to communicate unambiguously. Documenting choreography soon became a fruitless undertaking. About a decade later, in teaching Israeli dancers how to dance with a partner, I organized the hundreds of pointers I had learned into the three categories of balance, connection, and direction. Once categorized, I could see the many pointers in each category logically followed one overriding principle for that category. For example, no pushing and pulling is a logical consequence of the law of balance, everyone maintains their own balance. The laws of balance, connection, and direction follow both from the process of induction from the pointers in their categories, as well as from the process of deduction. Once you state the problem that you want to communicate unambiguously, you are led inextricably to the law of balance. Since everyone pushes and pulls different amounts at different times, you must eliminate pushing and pulling if you want to communicate unambiguously. Therefore everyone maintains their own balance. Once you have the law of balance, you need a way to define the position of the woman. You need a way to get the woman to move. You can then deduce the law of connection. Lastly, you can deduce the law of direction from the need to explain the woman's movement after initiated. Through observation of social dancing, you can work out the details.

Limit of Choreography, Step and Rotate

The communication is only concerned with the man communicating the woman's choreography. The woman is required to keep one foot on the floor to keep the law of balance. The only two movements the woman can make are step and rotate. Therefore we only need to consider communicating the choreography the woman can do by stepping and rotating.

Woman's Initial Position Is at (0,0) Facing (0,1)

Consider the dance floor as a plane with X and Y coordinates. Before the man leads anything, the woman's initial position is at (0,0) facing (0,1).

Stepping Facing Forward in 8 Directions

The woman can step with her free foot in any of 8 directions while facing in the (0,1) direction. The 8 directions are left (-1,0), right (1,0), forward (0,1), backward (0,-1) and at any angle on the four diagonals between each of these four directions.

Rotating in 2 Directions

The woman can rotate over her standing leg in 2 directions. While starting facing forward in the (0,1) direction, she can rotate to her left towards (-1,0) and right (1,0).

Can Traverse Any Pattern

Since the only two things the woman can do is to step or rotate, she must be able to trace any pattern by a combination of stepping and rotating.

There Are 11 Possibilities

Standing in one place, the woman can step in say 8 directions. The woman can also rotate to her left or to her right. Lastly, the woman can stay put, neither stepping nor rotating. This gives 11 possibilities.

All 11 Can Be Communicated Unambiguously

All 11 of these possibilities can be communicated unambiguously by following the laws of balance, connection, and direction. The man moves the connection either in a line in one of the eight directions or around the woman to the left or right to initiate her step or rotation. The communication is unambiguous because to maintain her frame, the woman can only move in one of the 10 directions or remain where she is.

The Length Is Defined

All that is left is to define how far the woman goes. Following the law of direction, the woman continues stepping or rotating in the direction indicated. To communicate the length, the man positions the connection where he wants the woman to stop. By returning to her frame, the woman can only be in one position at the end of her movement. Any length of either movement, step or rotate, is possible. Therefore, all 10 movements of any length, plus staying put, can be led unambiguously using the method in this book.

Combinations of Step and Rotate

A single dance combination consists of first stepping then rotating. The number of possibilities for a single, combination is then 9 step directions, including not stepping, times 3 rotation directions, including not rotating, which is 27 combinations. When the woman only steps and does not rotate, the 9 step directions are led as above. When the woman only rotates and does not step, the 3 rotation directions are led as above. When the woman steps and rotates, the man first initiates the woman's step direction, then initiates the woman's rotation direction. The man positions the connection where he wants her movement to end. He then first stops the rotation direction and then the step direction. Since the woman returns to her frame at the end, there is only one position in which she can finish. Therefore all 27 combinations of any length can be led unambiguously using the method in this book.

Figures Are Made Up of Four Basic Patterns

Logically then, there are three basic patterns of any length. The woman can step only, which is going straight. The woman can rotate only, which is turning. The woman can step and rotate, which is turn while traveling. All figures must be made of these three basic patterns since step and rotate are the only two movements the woman can make. For convenience, the method in this book adds a fourth pattern to walk around in a circle. Including the circle, there are four basic patterns.

The circle is a variation of going straight, which adds four more directions: circle around your partner to the left and right, and circle away from and back to your partner to the left and right. After adding 4 to the 9 directions for stepping, we have 13 stepping directions times 3 rotating directions. This gives 52 combinations of directions for the four basic patterns of any length for the woman. The circle is led by convention. You have to teach the woman when to walk around in a circle. Once the woman knows when to walk around in a circle, all 52 combinations can be led by the method in this book.

The Method Is Testable

You may not agree with my reasoning. The proof of any theory is in the practice. The method in this book is testable. I have successfully tested the method on more than 30 social dances with countless pieces of choreography. However, no one can make a satisfactory test of their own work.

For you to test my method, we can play a game to see how likely the method is to work. The game is you pick some social dance choreography. I win if I show (1) how to lead that choreography using the method in this book, or (2) that your chosen choreography falls outside the scope of social dancing. You win otherwise.

We play this game a number of times. Say I win each time. How good of a proof is this for the method? There are two outcomes, I win or you win. Let us say there is a 50% chance of either outcome happening randomly. Let us say this 50% is reasonable because you pick choreography that you try to beat me with. If I win once, there is a 50% chance that this was only luck. If I win twice in a row, there is only a 25% chance that this was luck. If I win ten times in a row, there is only a 1 in 1024 chance that this was luck. After 20 times, there is less than a 1 in one-million chance that this was luck.

You might argue, as my nephew Josh did, that the odds are not 1 out of 2. That the method odds are 90% likely to work. That we should be raising 90%, not 50%, to the power. You would be conceding that the method works 90% of the time. You would concede that we are only testing 10% of the most challenging choreography that you specifically select with which to win our game. However, the percentage does not matter. All that changes is the number of tests. At 90% odds, if I win 10 times in a row, there is about a 35% likelihood of that happening randomly. You would have to test 30 times to get to 4%. You would have to test 70 times to get to an uncertainty of 1 in a thousand. As long as I keep winning, at some point, you have to acknowledge that the test is sufficient for social dancing.

Points To Remember

1. The method of communicating in this book is testable.

Rules List

For Andrew Weitzen's How To Dance With a Partner

The following logical elements build one on top of the other. The sections are in order of importance. The purpose is more important than the objective. Values are more important than laws. The elements within the sections are also in order of importance. The law of balance takes precedence over the law of connection, which takes precedence over the law of direction.

Overview

Purpose: Help everyone enjoy themselves

Definitions: Clarify the meaning of the terminology

Objective: Two people dancing as one to the music

Social Values: Safety, courtesy, comfort

Dance Values: Natural, freedom, teamwork

Requirements: Clearly defined, easy, fast, universal

Responsibilities: The man keeps time with the music, positions the couple, and initiates the woman's movement. The woman keeps time with the man, maintains the connection, and completes her movement.

Laws: Everyone maintains their own balance. The woman maintains the connection. The woman maintains her direction.

Rules: The woman maintains her frame when the man moves the connection horizontally; the directions are straight, turn, circle

Corollary Highlights: Implications from preceding principles

Purpose

Purpose: Help everyone enjoy themselves when they go social dancing.

Definitions

Definition of Closed Position: The man and woman form an embrace on the man's right and the woman's left side.

Definition of Closed Position Close Embrace: In body contact.

Definition of Closed Position Open Embrace: Not in body contact.

Definition of Closed Position Closed Side: The side with the embrace, the man's right side and the woman's left side.

Definition of Closed Position Open Side: The side opposite the closed side, the man's left side and the woman's right side.

Definition of Complete Step: You finish your step balanced over your supporting leg.

Definition of Frame: The shape of your arms and torso.

Definition of Free Position: Any position when the man and woman are not touching one another.

Definition of Horizontal Movements: When keeping one foot on the floor, there are only two horizontal movements you can make, step and rotate.

Definition of Incomplete Step: You finish your step without being balanced over your supporting leg.

Definition of Off-Balance: You are unable to maintain your proper position by yourself.

Definition of Open Position: Any physically connected position that is not closed by the embrace.

Definition of Performance Choreography: Any choreography that is not social dance choreography.

Definition of the Physical Connection: The physical parts in contact with your partner.

Definition of Rotate: Rotating to change facing direction without changing weight.

Definition of Social Dancing: Dancing that puts the social nature of dancing first.

Definition of Social Dance Choreography: Any choreography you can unambiguously communicate safely without having practiced with your partner.

Definition of Step: Transfer of weight from one foot to another in one linear movement.

Definition of the Unit of Communication: The man invites the woman to move. The woman completes her movement. The man waits for her to finish.

Definition of the Visual Connection: The imaginary physical connection at a distance midway between the dance partners.

Definition of the Woman's Line of Dance: The line on which the woman dances.

See the Appendix topic Terminology for a complete list of definitions.

Objective

Objective of Partner Dancing: Two people dancing as one to the music.

Objective of Social Dancing: Have fun.

Social Values

Safety: Safety first, do not hurt yourself or anyone else.

Courtesy: Be respectful, do not tell anyone else what to do.

Comfort: Be physically and emotionally comfortable, say what you need.

Dance Values

Teamwork: The man invites and the woman completes.

Natural: Be natural.

Freedom: Maximize freedom of movement.

Communication Requirements

Clearly Defined: The communication is unambiguous.

Easy: Dancing should be easy enough for a normal person to do.

Fast: The communication must be fast enough to do in time to the music.

Universal: You use the same signals with every person in every dance.

Man's Responsibilities

The man's job is to be responsible for the couple as a whole.

1. Keep time with the music.

2. Position the couple on the dance floor.

3. Initiate the woman's movement.

Woman's Responsibilities

The woman's job is to follow the man.

1. Keep time with the man.

2. Maintain the connection.

3. Complete her movement.

Laws

Law of Balance: Everyone maintains their own balance.

Law of Connection: The woman maintains the connection.

Law of Direction: The woman maintains her direction.

Rules

Rule of Closing to Close Embrace: When the man presents his frame to invite the woman to a close embrace, the woman completes the embrace by positioning herself in body contact with the man.

Appendix

Rule of Closing to Open Embrace: When the man places his right hand on the woman's left shoulder blade, the woman places her left hand on the front of the man's right shoulder to complete the open embrace.

Rule of Connection Making and Breaking: The man chooses when to make and break the connection.

Rule of Connection Presentation: When the man presents a connection, he invites the woman to connect.

Rule of Direction: The three directions are straight, turn, and circle.

Rule of Following in Closed Position: The woman follows the connection she made with the man's body.

Rule of Frame: When the man moves the connection horizontally the woman maintains her frame. Otherwise, the woman allows her frame to adjust.

Rule of Frame with the Law of Connection: The woman maintains the connection by maintaining her frame when the man moves the connection horizontally. Otherwise, the woman allows her frame to adjust.

Rule of Leading in Closed Position: The man leads with the connection on his body.

Rule of Mirroring: When not physically connected, the woman follows by mirroring the man.

Rule of Plane of Communication: Horizontal communication is for horizontal movement. Vertical communication is for vertical movement.

Rule of Releasing from Closed Position: The woman releases her body connection when the man breaks the open embrace.

Rule of Stepping Backward: Whoever is moving backward is responsible for not getting their foot stepped on.

Rule of Visual Connection: Whenever there is no physical connection the woman maintains a visual connection.

Rule of Woman's Free Foot: The man is responsible for the woman's free foot.

Rule of Woman Stopping: The woman stops when her motion is blocked or she reaches the end of her connection.

Corollary Highlights

1. No pushing and pulling, not even a little.

2. Everyone does their own dancing.

3. Everyone moves their own body parts.

4. The woman's frame and the connection define the position of the woman.

5. Moving the woman's frame defines the initial movement of the woman to step or rotate in a particular direction.

6. Motion means to move. Stillness means stay still.

7. To lead a move, the man moves the connection horizontally.

8. To invite the woman to step, the man moves the connection in the direction he wants her to step.

9. To invite the woman to turn, the man moves the connection around the woman in the direction he wants her to turn.

10. The basic patterns are go straight, turn in place, walk around in a circle, and turn while traveling.

11. Stay on your line.

12. Go straight, turn, finish going straight.

13. You go from frame to spaghetti arms, and back to frame.

Rules Pocket Cards

ABCDs for How To Dance With a Partner
Attitude: Safety, everyone does their own dancing. Courtesy, do not tell anyone what to do. Comfort, say what you need. Teamwork, natural, freedom, clearly defined, easy, fast, universal.
Balance: Everyone maintains their own balance. No force.
Connection: The woman maintains the connection. She maintains her frame when the connection moves horizontally.
Direction: The woman maintains her direction: straight, turn, circle. Stop when blocked or at the end of the connection. Go straight, turn, finish going straight. Stay on your line.
Man: Keep time with the music. Position the couple. Initiate the woman's movement.
Woman: Keep time with the man. Complete her movement.

ABCDs for How To Dance With a Partner
Attitude: Safety, everyone does their own dancing. Courtesy, do not tell anyone what to do. Comfort, say what you need. Teamwork, natural, freedom, clearly defined, easy, fast, universal.
Balance: Everyone maintains their own balance. No force.
Connection: The woman maintains the connection. She maintains her frame when the connection moves horizontally.
Direction: The woman maintains her direction: straight, turn, circle. Stop when blocked or at the end of the connection. Go straight, turn, finish going straight. Stay on your line.
Man: Keep time with the music. Position the couple. Initiate the woman's movement.
Woman: Keep time with the man. Complete her movement.

Copyright (c) 2007, 2022 by Andrew Weitzen. All rights reserved.
www.PartnerDancing.com

Appendix

Rules Summary
ABCDs for How To Dance With a Partner
Social Dancing: Dancing that puts the social nature of dancing first.
Objective: Two people dancing as one to the music.
Social Dance Choreography: Any move you can unambiguously communicate safely without having practiced with your partner.

Attitude
Safety: Safety first, do not hurt yourself or anyone else. No force.
Courtesy: Be respectful, do not tell anyone else what to do.
Comfort: Be comfortable, say what you need.
Teamwork: The man invites and the woman completes.
Natural: How people naturally move and interact.
Freedom: Maximize freedom of movement.
Clearly Defined: Logical, precise, unambiguous communication.
Easy: Simple enough for a normal person to learn.
Fast: Fast enough to communicate in time to music.
Universal: Works the same with everyone for every dance.

Balance: Everyone maintains their own balance. Everyone does their own dancing. Everyone moves their own body parts. Maintain your posture. No pushing and pulling.
Connection: The woman maintains the connection. The woman maintains her frame when the connection moves sideways. At all other times, the woman lets her frame adjust.
Direction: The woman maintains her direction: straight, turn, circle. Stops when blocked or at the end of the connection. Go straight, turn, finish going straight. Stay on your line.

Man's Responsibilities: Keep time with the music. Position the couple on the dance floor. Initiate the woman's movement.
Woman's Responsibilities: Keep time with the man. Complete her movement.

Terminology

This terminology is specific to this author.

Balanced: You are able to maintain your proper position by yourself.

Ballroom Dancing: Professionally organized dancing based on one of the ballroom dance associations. This consists of both social and performance dancing. Includes around a dozen dances, categorized into rhythm and smooth. The dances may include bolero, cha-cha, foxtrot, jive, mambo, quick-step, pasodoble, rumba, samba, tango, Viennese waltz, and waltz.

Basic Patterns: The four patterns that makeup all the figures for the woman. They are go straight, turn in place, walk around in a circle, and turn while traveling.

Choreographed Dancing: Any dancing that is pre-choreographed.

Circle or Walk Around in a Circle: Walk around in a circle either around or away from and back to your partner. One of four basic patterns for the woman.

Circle Signal: Move the connection to start the woman walking in a circle.

CLOD: Couple's line of dance.

Closed Position: The couple is in an embrace. Closed position is characterized by the woman making contact with the man's body.

Closed Position Close Embrace: A closed position in body contact.

Closed Position Closed Side: The man's right side and the woman's left side.

Closed Position Open Embrace: A closed position without body contact.

Closed Position Open Side: The man's left side and the woman's right side.

Complete Step: You finish your step balanced over your supporting foot.

Connection: The physical points of contact between the dance partners.

Couple's Line of Dance: The line between the couple's on which their mutual center moves.

Direction Signal: The man moves the connection to signal the woman to go straight, turn, or circle.

Embrace: The man's right arm is around the woman. The woman's left hand or arm are on or around the man's body. The embrace is characterized by the woman making a connection with the man's body.

Figures: Structured choreography for the woman made up of the basic patterns. Common choreography taught in dance classes.

Folk Dancing: Dances taken from ethnic people. Folk dances are usually done by folk dance groups. The dances are usually choreographed.

Follower: In couples dancing, the partner who follows the leader. In group dances, any person following a leader.

Frame: The shape of your arms to your body.

Free Foot or Leg: The foot or leg that is ready to move and bears no weight.

Free Position: Any position when the man and woman are not touching one another.

Go Straight: Walk on a straight line. One of four basic patterns for the woman.

Go Straight Signal: Move the connection in a straight line in the direction for the woman to go.

Group Dancing: Any dance that can have more than two people doing the same dance together. One person can do a group dance alone.

Gumby: A rubber, toy humanoid figure with a wireframe that is flexible but rebounds back into position if not stretched too far.

Horizontal Sensation: The feeling of motion in the woman to step or rotate.

Incomplete Step: You finish your step without your weight balanced over the foot to which you stepped.

Lead and Follow: A means of communicating in which one person leads and the other person follows.

Leader: The person leading the dance, either in a partner or group dance.

Line of Dance: The line around the room in which people travel while dancing, usually counter-clockwise.

LOD: Line of dance.

Man: The leader. Used for ease of reading to allow for the use of the pronoun he. Anyone of any gender can dance either role.

Off-Balance: Any time you are unable to maintain your proper position by yourself.

One: Proposed term to replace leader.

Open Position: Any physically connected position that is not a closed position. Open positions are when the partners are touching, but not in an embrace.

Partial Step: You finish your step with your weight on your foot, but your body is not balanced over your foot.

Partner Dancing: Any dancing done with a partner.

PDL^{SM}: Partner dance language.

Performance Choreography: Choreography that is not social dance choreography.

Performance Dancing: Dancing that requires practicing with a partner beforehand.

Recreational Dancing: Any dancing done for recreation.

Rotate: Change of facing direction without the transfer of weight. One of the only two movements the woman can make. The other is step.

Social Dancing: Dancing that puts the social nature of dancing first.

Social Dance Choreography: Any choreography you can unambiguously communicate safely without having practiced with your partner.

Step: Transfer of weight from one foot to another in one linear movement. One of the only two movements the woman can make. The other is rotate.

Supporting Foot or Leg: Foot or leg that bears your weight.

Tin Man: A man made of tin from the Wizard of Oz, with a movable, but rigid, metal frame with no give.

Turn in Place: Turn, ending in the same position, possibly facing a new direction. One of four basic patterns for the woman.

Turn Signal: Move the connection around the woman in the direction for her to turn.

Turn While Traveling: Turn while going straight or circling, continuing to step in the same direction. One of four basic patterns for the woman.

Visual Connection: The imaginary point of contact between the dance partners when not physically connected.

Two: Proposed term to replace follower.

WLOD: Woman's line of dance.

Woman: The follower. Used for ease of reading to allow for the use of the pronoun she. Anyone of any gender can dance either role.

Woman's Base Frame: The default frame for the woman.

Woman's Line of Dance: The line on which the woman dances when she is going straight or circling.

Voices

The following people have provided voices for the audio version of this book.

Randi Faris as Edith Weitzen, her mother
Andrew Weitzen as all other voices and the narrator
Soojin Yoo as herself

What Others Have To Say

The most important thing you learn is how to get along with others at social dancing.

> Andy, would you dance with me. I was in a car accident. I do not move well. You dance so gently. You are one of the only ones that I feel safe with. ~ Deborah, contra dancer

When you learn how to dance without the use of force, everyone can feel safe dancing with you.

> At West Coast swing, one lady said, "You are so easy to dance with. You dance so softly. All the other guys are rough."

You learn how to dance gently so you are a pleasure to dance with. When you dance this way, these are the kind of sentiments you hear wherever you go.

This comment was posted on a folk dance forum in response to a friendly exchange. "Wow, it sounds like a whole lot of rules. Is there any punishment for the disobedient? :))".

> Actually, there are no rules at all, just good physiology and good physics, as well as politeness, personal responsibility, and common sense. I have been dancing Israeli and international, contra, swing, and ballroom, for over 20 years. Andy's classes are the only ones where I do not get hurt--pushed, pulled, jerked, stepped on, or thumb wrestled.
>
> He is the only teacher I have ever had who does not teach only moves, patterns, and choreography, but instead has worked out a few basic principles that apply

to all types of dancing. No punishment, only pleasure. ~ Erin, recreational dancer

One man wrote the following note after attending the Chagigah Israeli dance camp in Wisconsin.

Andy,

A markida [woman dance leader] from out of town recently told me that it was a pleasure to dance with me, that I did not break her arm, and that I was very gentle. This was music to my ears, as I have been working on dancing safely and comfortably, without any pushing or pulling, ever since I attended one of your workshops a few years ago.

Within the same week, I learned that two other dancers with whom I dance frequently were also complemented during a dance camp this past weekend. They were both women who were complemented on their following skills, and one of them was complemented by a markid [man dance leader] with whom she danced. I dance frequently with both of these women, and we work together on skills that you taught at your workshop in Mount Prospect, IL.

I am very pleased that people are starting to realize the benefits of dancing safely, and these experiences are a real testament to your teaching and mine.

~ Jeff, social dancer

One woman had written to me that she thought the swing dance class "was very good--and everyone we spoke with thought the same". I wrote her back asking what she liked specifically. This is her reply.

Andy,

The simplicity of the breaks (movements without a lot of steps), while feeling and practicing the lead, broke it down in a way that was extremely useful. We were able to focus on the lead and follow while not trying to learn a complex dance.

Another thing we found really useful was closing our eyes to get the feel of the lead. You had done that in another of your classes. A lot of us were dancing with our ordinary partners and that drill is useful so that we do not just watch body language.

Also, ending the evening with Bala was great. It gave us all some dancing that was fun and a chance to dance with everyone. It ends the evening on a positive note and shows that dancing really is fun!

~ Annette, social dancer

Annette and her partner Randy now run their own weekly English country dance session. Often, they are invited to be guest leaders in other cities. Everyone at their sessions dances gently.

More Comments

All the comments here were unsolicited. All the comments were written except for the one from my mother. The author made minor editorial changes for readability, such as removing blank lines and correcting spelling. The author was reluctant to change punctuation because that would require too much editing of the original notes. The author prefers the reader see the comments as expressed by the commenter. The author removed irrelevant paragraphs such as those asking about when a class might be given. The author did not add any words to the comments. The author added the attribution after the name so you can see the commenter's background. The author's notes are in square brackets. Some names have been changed.

Hi Andy,

You are such a devoted person to build the community (of all dances) :)

~ Andrea, Argentine tango instructor

* * *

Hi Andy,

Dance class was soooo much fun. Nice job in corralling all of us wild dancers.

~ Angie Ferkovich, social dancer and organizer

* * *

Hi Andy,

I just wanted to say thank you, again, for coming to our 1940s party and making it special with your dancing know-how! Everyone had a wonderful time, especially the birthday girls. Thanks so much for the wonderful music and your time and effort. Best,

~ Anita, beginning swing dancer

What Others Have To Say

* * *

Hi Andy!

I love the tango music and I know lots of other people would like the classes. Again, I thank you for setting up the classes!

~ Ann, recreational dancer

* * *

Hi Andy,

It really was an especially enjoyable evening. Many thanks for your hard work and patience.

~ Arlene, Israeli and international folk dancer

* * *

Another WOW! You are the best and thanks again for the information. I hope the Tango class can continue in April.

~ Carmelo, beginning social dancer

* * *

Thanks, Andy, for the encouragement. You are the best. Your guidelines are sooooooo helpful. I am saving your comprehensive guidelines for frequent reference and reminder.

~ Carol, recreational dancer

Appendix

* * *

Thanks for putting together the West Coast swing classes. I had some people after class tonight mentioning how much they enjoyed it. You did a good job.

~ Cathy, West Coast swing competitor

* * *

Hi Andy,

What a great class! Thanks! It was so nice to meet new people.

~ Cheri Ruiz, recreational dancer

* * *

Hi Andy,

It was a pleasure meeting you on Thursday at Victor and Oksana's milonga in Boca Raton. I enjoyed dancing with you so much, I only wish I could have danced with you more that night. You are a very good dancer. Whenever you are in Boca again, please let me know. Enjoy the rest of your weekend and I look forward to hearing from you.

Thanks,
~ Cindy, Argentine tango dancer

What Others Have To Say

* * *

Hi Andy,

I want to thank you for the time and motivation you put into the Israeli dancing. It is certainly a blessing for many.

~ Cindy, Israeli dancer

* * *

Thank you Andrew for what you are doing.

~ Cindy, social dancer

* * *

Thank you so much, Andy, for your welcoming nature!

~ Connie, line dancer

* * *

Thank you, Andy,

You are so right. Excellent advice. I need this reminder. Love,

~ Cyd, recreational dancer

* * *

You are one of the best things that ever happened to the Mosaics [outdoor clubs where I led dancing at their international event].

~ David Liebman, recreational dancer

Appendix

* * *

Hi Andy,

I love your values and am so envious that you have this going on in Florida. Thanks for the encouragement, though. Keep up the wonderful work you do and come visit us again!

~ Diane, folk dancer

* * *

Thank you for the update Andy. Is appreciated. As is your tireless efforts to find all of us a place to continue dancing. I hope you will join us this Sunday at waltz brunch.

~ Don Page, vintage waltz and zydeco dance organizer

* * *

Do they pay you?

~ Edith Weitzen, social dancer and my mother

* * *

Hi Andy,

Dancing last night was, in my opinion, wonderful. I was so energized when I got home, it was almost like being high. You are very good at leading a group. You are welcoming, have a good sense of pacing, you encourage without being too pushy, correct without giving offense.

~ Erin, social dancer

What Others Have To Say

* * *

Dear Andy,

I am in the final stages of packing for my move to Atlanta and Stone Mountain. I would have said goodbye in person, but we have a pandemic. You have had a tremendous impact on my health and happiness and I will be forever grateful. I met you at a time that I was fearful and in considerable pain from loss. Your dance class let me feel safe with strangers and specifically safe with men. Your teaching is excellent and the atmosphere of welcome and respect for all that you foster is unmatched. With dance in general and tango in particular, you opened a community and world to me that has greatly enriched my life. You have led gently and confidently in each dance and in the whole expansion into the world of dance.

I am confident that I will see you again someday at some milonga somewhere and I will be glad. I wish you the very best in all things because that is what you give and that is what you deserve in return.

~ Sincerely, Frida, social dancer

* * *

Hi Andrew,

You are a terrific teacher and it was wonderful reliving my youthful dance experiences. Best regards,

~ Gale, Israeli dancer

Appendix

* * *

Thank you for sharing your wisdom. I find your notes very insightful and useful.

~ Iris, Argentine tango dancer

* * *

Hi Andy,

Thanks for the information and for the lovely dances.

~ Jackie, Argentine tango dancer

* * *

Andy,

Really love working with you and want to continue to get lessons.

~ Jennifer, hustle dancer

* * *

Hi Andy,

Thank you. And Joseph. You guys taught a great class today. It was a lot of fun and my students absolutely loved it! Again thank you for two wonderful classes.

~ Juliana, University of Florida professor of dance, dance professional, Brazilian dance instructor

What Others Have To Say

* * *

Hello Andy,

I was driving back to Gainesville from Waldo yesterday and saw your sign GainesvilleDance.com. Did a double-U on the road, parked on the side, and took a photo of the sign. Congratulations, great sign! Thanks for promoting dance. You are doing a great job. Gainesville is a dance city, very much so.

~ Julieta, international folk dancer teacher

* * *

Dear B'nai Israel Board Members:

I want to express to you my feelings about the importance of the Israeli Dance program at B'nai Israel. That is because Andy Weitzen is willing to single-handedly put in the energy needed to make it happen. He provides his own music and equipment, he writes a weekly newsletter for local Israeli Dancing, and most importantly, he consistently dedicates his Monday evening each week to running the program, providing a warm environment and genuine expertise for everyone who comes. He patiently teaches and re-teaches us the dances, always able to expand our dance horizons because he knows so many dances. It is a great service that Andy provides to our community.

Respectfully,
~ Karen, Israeli dancer

Appendix

* * *

I liked what you wrote about safety, courtesy and comfort!! See you tonight! Salsa too?

~ Kathie, social and Israeli dancer [married her husband who she got to know in my class]

* * *

Andy,

Last night was very fun! And Jeff and I are delighted you will continue with two-step in January.

~ Kathryn, social dancer [met her husband in my class]

* * *

Hi Andy,

Saturday was fun. Thanks for playing some ballroom music and for getting me into the swing rueda. I probably never would have tried it otherwise!

~ Kay, instructor and recreational dancer

* * *

As always thank you and I am holding you to your word. Everyone learns to dance!!!!!!. Enjoyed waltz immensely; more waltz lessons.

~ Kellyann Curnayn, social dancer [met her significant other in my class]

What Others Have To Say

* * *

Hi Andy,

Just wanted to say that I thought you taught an EXCELLENT class in all ways in lindy hop tonight. I like the way you teach! VERY impressive your knowledge of the dance, and excellent the way you taught and broke down each part of each step for both lead and follower - such that by the end of tonight's class - some of the women who I do not think had danced this before were doing surprisingly good. The last song you played in the swing rueda was fairly fast - and many of the followers were keeping up to the speed. I like the technique you taught. I had done a cross behind (with my right foot) on 5 - rather than a step straight (to the right) down the aisle - but your technique seems far simpler - and I found I was able to "open the door" to get the woman swinging out rapidly without any force on my part at all (Nicely worded by you - and nicely demonstrated). After that, it became easy to "rebuild" steps (free spin, inside turn) - and it was "coming back to me". I do not think I have ever felt as unhurried and relaxed doing swing outs as you had me feeling by the end of the night.

A few suggestions/thoughts: Thanks for helping after class with Juliet. I had never met her before - and she overall was really getting the hang of everything - except the 180 degree turn on 3, which made the dance uncomfortable (because she was facing the wrong way). Very helpful that you identified her need not to break her right shoulder so that she would turn on 3 - and also helpful to me to understand how she was already by me on 2 negating any possibility for me to get her to turn unless I did something else to compensate.

You taught an EXCELLENT class in swing-out, with success at getting virtually everyone doing the step to reasonably fast music which is no small feat. You also were great at refreshing what I had forgotten and not used for at least 3 years. THANK YOU! :)

~ Ken, social dancer

* * *

Andy,

I wanted to email you and let you know how much I appreciate your support for the dance, for supporting Annette and Randy and for being someone who is a pleasure to dance with, no matter what the dance form! I love being at the GDMA [Gainesville Dance and Music Association] building, it had gone away before I started coming to Gainesville to dance and I like the atmosphere and the floor in the room we use. So, this is my way of saying thank you very much for all you are doing to support dance in the Gainesville area.

~ Liza, social dancer

* * *

Thanks Andy,

I was just curious, how you are teaching all the variety dances [online]. So, I just wanted to check out your site this week, and peeking a little bit of the other dances, like Israeli dance, etc. Just curious.

After looking at your class, I started thinking of going back to the beginner ballroom classes of our community to learn the lead role. (Still, Maybe?) Since the number of female dancers are more than the male, If I can dance it, I can have some fun by myself with my female friends. Of course, this (my idea) is going to be after the pandemic lock down ended.

Sometimes, I get tired of the slow progress of Argentine Tango. There are so many expectations of flexibility which is hard for our not-so-young age. There are many No, No, Nos too. So, it seems that the easy simple dances like you are teaching, might be a good break for me.

Anyway, you have been giving me some inspiration! Thank you!

~ M. S., Argentine tango and social dancer

* * *

Andy,

I am very happy to receive this invitation as it represents the best of collaborative effort for dancing. Thanks so very much for all you have accomplished and for being a central nerve.

~ Marilyn, ballroom and social dancer

* * *

Dear Andy,

I had a magnificent time last night. Thank you so very much for enabling us ladies to dance with you virtually. You are an extremely hard worker. Again, many thanks,

~ Margaret, ballroom and social dancer

Appendix

* * *

Dear Andy,

We very much enjoyed the swing dance class today. As always, you are so patient and calm, and make us feel very comfortable.

~ Marsha and Teo, Argentine tango instructors

* * *

Andy,

Thank you so much for your patience at the swing dance. Sharing the info today was very helpful. May you continue all your activities. You are a very kind and knowledgeable person. All the best to you. Sincerely

~ Mary Ann, social dancer

* * *

Hiya Andy,

That was a pretty good turnout Saturday night, thanks to you and Ann for making it work.

~ Metin, social dancer

* * *

Cool, I will see if she will let me in this week. I like your approach to other teachers.

~ Michael, contra dancer

What Others Have To Say

* * *

Hi Andrew,

Thank you for sending me the newsletters. I really appreciated the list of line dances you have been doing with the links to videos. It has been a few years for me to restart dancing. I found most of your dances are new to me. It is exciting to learn new dances in your class at the senior center. Happy holiday and Happy New Year,

~ Mitch, line dancer

* * *

I went to [another dance class] last night. I will go this month, but please hurry and come back. I like the way you teach it better. I am finding their method very difficult. I have been spoiled by Andy! We did salsa last night which was okay, but I stayed for the 2 step advanced lesson and even though you had taught us this particular move, I struggled to follow their method. They spend a lot of time teaching the follower steps and you have to visualize being led. I found that difficult. Oh well good practice. Have a wonderful time and bring back a lifetime of memories!

[sometime later] As usual a great class. I like the combination of the 4 different dances as the footwork changes it forces me to rely on my lead and focus on learning to follow. I will practice bringing my feet together! Can't practice the hand and frame without a partner! Have a great week and I will see you next Monday. I may try to go to waltz on Sunday if I get back in town on Saturday. See ya!

~ Oel Wingo, social dancer

Appendix

* * *

I am thankful that I signed up for your class last fall. The music and dances are great. It is fun to meet new people and to develop friendships with people who continue to come because of a common love for the dances. I found it more difficult than I expected since each song has a different dance. However your patience and encouragement have been amazing.

In addition to all of this, I have been helped physically more than I dreamed possible. My doctor approved me taking the class in spite of the diagnosis of degenerative disk disease. What he does not know yet is the fact that I am no longer taking the prescription strength Ibuprofen that I had taken four years prior to starting to dance. Of course, he was prescribing a medication to protect my digestive system. I have stopped it too. Since I had tried to stop the Ibuprofen before without success, I know that it was dancing that made the difference.

One night a week and some practice between classes helped improve my posture and motivated me to do other exercises as well. I am definitely in better health now than I was last September. Thanks for the part that you played in that change. I hope that you will continue to teach dance for years to come. Thanks,

~ Pat, Israeli dancer

What Others Have To Say

* * *

Dear Andy,

I have so enjoyed the Line Dancing Class and am so disappointed that I am unable to sign up for the March Session. I will miss three of the four sessions in March so it makes no sense for me to sign up. I will also be out of town the first two weeks in April. It has been such fun-- I have really enjoyed it and hope to rejoin sometime in the future. Happy Dancing,

~ Peggy, line dancer

* * *

Hi Andy!

Annette and I had a great time, as usual, dancing with you last night. And I have to say, I really admire your patience! It cannot be easy to stay so calm and collected when some are (rudely) questioning what you are trying to teach. Good job!

~ Randy, English country dance instructor

Appendix

**

Yep, your methods definitely work! It was fun to feel like I was actually dancing (vs. just being dragged around the dance floor). Maybe it takes a little more concentration to follow, but it beats having to learn the whole dance first. Lots more fun your way. (And hey, if you can teach me, you can teach anyone!)

Do not let me forget - I have another question for you about spinning in the circle dances - how not to get dizzy? See you!

Ricki

[next email]

I went to the last hour of the Bolton Center dance - the spins worked great! I could tell my partners were much more comfortable. Definitely worth the time to learn it. Thanks!

~ Ricki, contra, folk, and social dancer

**

You are a generous gifted dancer that shares his skills and graces with partners of all levels. Hugs,

~ Rosanna, Argentine tango dancer

What Others Have To Say

* * *

Thanks Andy,

I attended the class Thursday evening, and was relieved that you are taking it so slow! I really appreciated your comments about how long it takes to develop the muscle memory! My previous attempts to learn to dance with a partner were just an embarrassing failure. But I have seen folks having so much fun dancing that I wanted to try again when I heard about this class. So here is hoping!

~ Ruby, beginning social dancer

* * *

Hi Andy,

Thank you so much for making our event even more special. You really got people up and moving and the "spectators" enjoyed watching! I had fun myself! You were great to work with and I hope you will join us for many future events.

~ Sharon, President of the Jewish Council of North Central Florida 2014

* * *

Andy,

Even more important, I want to thank you for your motivating and supportive teaching. You are great!!

~ Ted, social dancer

Appendix

**

Hi Andy,

Thanks for all your efforts, past and present, to keep dance alive in Gainesville!!

~ Theresa, Argentine tango, swing, and social dancer

**

Hi Andrew,

Your site is good! You are brilliant and tough to keep all dancing despite Covid! Thank you for your skills. Your Pal,

~ Tom, social dancer

**

Dear Andrew,

What an enjoyable night of dancing on Sunday! A little bit of everything: oldies, newer dances, couples, and something new. All in a relaxed, friendly atmosphere. You are so good at managing the group and accommodating everyone who shows up.

~ Veronica, Israeli dance instructor and English country dance caller